JUVENILE JUSTICE AND INJUSTICE

JUVENILE JUSTICE AND INJUSTICE

MARGARET O. HYDE

FRANKLIN WATTS
New York | London | Toronto | Sydney
REVISED EDITION | 1983

Library of Congress Cataloging in Publication Data

Hyde, Margaret Oldroyd, 1917-
Juvenile justice and injustice.

Bibliography: p.
Includes index.

Summary: Discusses the problems of the juvenile
justice system, case studies of youthful offenders,
and existing community programs that help them.
1. Juvenile justice, Administration of—United States
—Juvenile literature. 2. Juvenile courts
—United States—Juvenile literature. 3. Status
offenders—Legal status, laws, etc.—United States
—Juvenile literature. [1. Juvenile courts.
2. Juvenile delinquency. 3. Law] I. Title.
KF9780.H9   1983   345.73'08   82-20150
ISBN 0-531-04594-3   347.3058

CONTENTS

For
Helen B. Doremus,
D.V.M.
and
Henry M. Doremus,
D.V.M.

JUVENILE JUSTICE
AND INJUSTICE

1

JUVENILE JUSTICE UNDER ATTACK

The search for a better juvenile justice system continues as many different voices call for a wide variety of approaches. The media dwells on the plight of the public, the victims of violent juvenile offenders. But little is written about the plight of the nonviolent offenders—the children who need help from society more than society needs protection from them. These are the runaways, the habitual truants, the children whose parents cannot control them, and the alcohol and other drug abusers who become part of the juvenile justice system. Many of these children are placed in detention centers where they are mistreated.

Two important goals of the Juvenile Justice and Delinquency Prevention Act of 1974 were the removal of nondelinquents from secure facilities and the removal of all children from adult jails. While some headway has been made, the challenge still looms large. According to a 1981 report by the Community Research Center of the University of Illinois, approximately half a million juveniles in the

United States are locked up in adult jails each year while awaiting placement. Four percent of the juveniles jailed have not committed an offense of any sort, and 20 percent are detained for offenses such as underage drinking, sexual promiscuity, or running away. Over 9 percent of jailed juveniles are thirteen years old or younger.

Some action is being taken to get juveniles out of jail. The abuse suffered by juveniles in jail has been called the most serious of the nation's long-standing failures in the areas of out-of-home placement and incarceration. The old idea that a night in jail teaches a young person a lesson is quickly abandoned by those citizens who take the trouble to find out about the conditions in their local jails.

Many of the young people who are placed in jail to await their appearance in juvenile court suffer severe abuses. Some have their heads held in toilets; some are raped, beaten, or put in isolation. Sometimes isolation is an attempt to remove the juveniles from the "sight and sound" of adult offenders as prescribed by local law, but these good intentions do nothing to eliminate the emotional damage of isolation.

An amendment to the Juvenile Justice and Delinquency Prevention Act called for the development of new ways to deal with serious offenders. This group of juveniles who require incarceration reenter society with a commitment to crime. The majority of today's adult criminals have experienced incarceration as juveniles. How can the problem of juvenile violent crime be handled so that there is justice for the public as well as for the juvenile who grows up in a world where narcotics dealing, mugging, rape, and extortion are a part of normal life?

Our juvenile justice system is accused of being both too lenient and too harsh. Both accusations may be true, depending on the individual case. The system is under attack from many directions by those who have some knowledge of the way it works. Such attacks are helping to bring action, but the great majority of people have no idea of what is happening to young people in trouble.

What are the present functions of a juvenile court? Whether or not you know or ever will know someone who appears in the court, the problem of juvenile justice and injustice plays an important part in your life. Between those who live in fear of crime to those who commit crime (sometimes out of fear), there is a wide canyon. But those who criticize the courts for being too harsh or too lenient might reverse their opinions in some cases if they knew more of the facts.

When you see a newspaper picture of a boy or girl in trouble with the police, what goes through your mind? Has he or she committed murder or assault, stolen a car, picked a pocket, sold illegal drugs, vandalized a school, or just stayed away from one?

Thousands of the juvenile offenders who are taken into custody find their way into a system of training schools. These are places where they are supposed to receive treatment and rehabilitation, but which have long been referred to as training schools for crime. The boy or girl waiting at a detention or screening center will probably be sent to such a place. Other offenders go to ranches, forestry camps, and farms, where there is less confinement and greater contact with the local community. Halfway houses and group homes provide even more extensive contact with schools and community. What happens to most delinquents depends largely on the judge of juvenile court, who is usually struggling with a great overload of cases.

"What do I do with Joseph?" "What is the best for

Kim?" After hearing the report of the investigating officer, the judge usually must decide in a brief period of time. Seldom do Joseph or Kim have much to say.

Picture a boy named Jim who at fourteen years of age is a member of a gang whose territory includes part of the West Village of New York City. One night, Jim stabs a man, who dies as a result of the wound. When taken into custody, Jim pleads self-defense. But in the time between his arrest and the trial, Jim is permitted to go home in the custody of his mother. Neighbors complain that Jim is dangerous and should not be allowed freedom to roam the streets with his old gang. His mother could not stop this before. Can she influence Jim or exert better control of his action now?

If Jim is convicted, he may go to a training school or he may be held in some other kind of custody until he is twenty-one years old. Or he may convince the judge of his need to defend himself and be set free. Who speaks for the dead man? There could be a question of guilt.

Connie stands before a juvenile court judge after running away from home several times. Her mother says she cannot control Connie and expresses fear that her daughter may become pregnant. The mother asks the judge to send her daughter to a training school to "help her." The judge does so "for the girl's own good." The mother may or may not have some knowledge as to what happens at a typical training school, but she does know that she will be free of many problems at home if Connie leaves.

At the training school, Connie will be labeled a runaway or status offender, but the label will mean very little. There, she may join girls who have committed a wide variety of crimes. Since Connie feels unwanted at home and unworthy of love, she probably will not be very cooperative with the authorities at the training center. It may be a long time before she is free. She may learn how to commit crimes far more serious than running away, an action that would not be an offense if she were an adult.

Gary came to juvenile court on a charge of shoplifting after growing up in a twelve-room house in a California desert. A private swimming pool shone like a jewel in the sun and every possible comfort was provided. Gary was one boy among thousands who lived in houses that stretched for mile upon mile out over the canyon west to the sea. The only unpleasant part of his physical environment was the smog that backed up against the mountains so that on some days young children were not allowed on the school playground. But smog was not the only problem in Gary's life. His parents were divorced, something not unusual in the United States. About half the children in Gary's class came from families with single parents or stepparents. His family, before the divorce, had moved every two or three years from one town to another. Gary's mother worked at night, so he was free to join the group who met in someone's house to drink, smoke grass, and/or make love. Usually this started at three in the afternoon with beer and ended at midnight with a few joints to mellow out the evening. Gary's life was not uncommon among seventh graders in his set. He was one of the gang who would usually go on to "bigger and better things." He had already been in and out of trouble several times for throwing rocks at trucks, sniffing glue, experimenting with other drugs, stealing hubcaps, and shoplifting. This time, a promise of private psychiatric treatment set him free. His future would be uncertain but he was now free from juvenile court.

Twelve-year-old Julia was not so lucky. She grew up on the streets of a poverty area, where she indulged in petty crime much of the time. After she was brought into custody, no place could be found for her other than an institution for delinquent children. She probably needed psychiatric care as much as Gary, and certainly her crimes were no more severe. But there were no funds to supply such help, so she joined the army of children in a system of which it has been said, "A child trapped in the system has no hope."

Nancy was thirteen years old when she was first brought to a detention center for shoplifting. The detective at the department store where she pocketed some scarves tried to reach her parents but could not. So she was brought to the detention center. Here it was discovered that her mother was an alcoholic and her father had left home many years ago. Nancy fended for herself much of the time. She had written the letters of the word *hate* on the fingers of her left hand with a ball-point pen. After studying her background, the judge asked the probation officer to find a place for her in a foster home. It took several months before a place could be found.

If Nancy had just taken your wallet, you might feel the proper treatment would be to commit her to a few years in jail. But the law states that treatment should be in the best interest of the child. The judge must decide what is best for her, rather than exact punishment for her crime.

The young person who is delinquent is one of the greatest problems of our time. How to reduce street crime by juveniles and help them in such a way that they will no longer need or want to commit further street crimes is probably an unanswerable question. Juvenile courts deal with many different kinds of children who have committed antisocial offenses, and each one has a different set of circumstances. What began as an attempt to help children in trouble and to separate them from adult criminals is now considered society's dumping ground. Policemen have claimed that the children they bring into custody for serious offenses are discharged so quickly that they beat them home from court. People who have been violated by young offenders are asking for an end to what appears to be a revolving door system for criminals because they are under a certain age. Others decry the plight of children who are subjected to maltreatment of a kind that seems impossible in a so-called enlightened society. What can be done?

2

CHILDREN IN TROUBLE BEFORE THE DAYS OF JUVENILE COURT

What happens to youthful offenders today is a result of the ways children were treated through the centuries. The American system of juvenile justice came from the English methods of treating children in trouble. Picture some of those living in seventeenth-century England. Here are some actual case studies of children who broke the laws of England at that time:

In May of 1686, a boy of ten years of age was indicted for stealing thirty yards of lemon-colored satin ribbon. He was found coming to the house of the victim about ten o'clock at night where he pretended to buy a hatband. When he saw the desired piece of ribbon, he ran away with it, but he came back the next day. The maid saw him and caused him to be apprehended. The prisoner claimed he was going to the town of Rumford for a horse for his master and pretended that he knew nothing of the ribbon. He was found guilty and was ordered to be whipped.

On May 15, 1684, a girl named Jane Owen was indicted

for stealing a silver mustard pot and three silver spoons. She had impersonated a boy and entered the service of Mr. William Hanuay, waiting upon him as his boy until she had obtained a new suit of clothing. Then she ran away with the silver. Jane Owen was found guilty and was sentenced "to be burnt in the hand."

About the middle of the eighteenth century, records in London state the following:

> *In criminal cases, an infant at the age of 14 may be capitally punished for any capital offense, but under the age of 7 he cannot. The period between 7 and 14 is subject to much uncertainty. For the infant shall generally speaking be judged prima facie innocent; yet if he could discern between good and evil at the time of the offense committed, he may be convicted and receive judgment and execution of death though he hath not attained to years of puberty or discretion.*

Seven was the magic age at which children were believed to be able to tell the difference between right and wrong. From eight to fourteen, according to English common law, children could be held responsible for criminal acts if it could be shown that they were intelligent enough to understand the nature and consequences of what they had done. They could be subjected to the same type of trial and sentence as adults. In extreme cases they could suffer the death penalty, although many offenders were released because parents pleaded them too immature to commit a crime.

William Blackstone, who was an authority on English law in the late 1700s, cites several cases in which children between the ages of ten and thirteen were subjected to execution for murder or other crimes. In 1828, a thirteen-year-old boy was hanged in the state of New Jersey for an offense he committed when he was twelve years old. Such severe punishments were not common for children, but large numbers suffered severe treatment even for minor crimes. Young people were commonly sentenced to punishment by being burned on the hand, whipped, or transported from the country. Sentences were not always carried out.

Wiley B. Sanders, in his book *Juvenile Offenders for a Thousand Years,* cites the instance of a boy of ten who was convicted for the murder of a girl of five years of age in the year 1748. He received a sentence of death but the chief justice respited execution "out of regard to the tender years of the prisoner" till he had the opportunity of taking the opinion to other judges. The report of the case indicates that the boy and girl were under the care of a parishioner at whose house they were lodged and maintained. On the day of the murder, the parishioner and his wife went out to work early in the morning and left the children in bed together. When they returned from work, the girl was missing and the boy was asked where she was. He answered that he had helped her up, put on her clothes, that she had gone away and that he did not know where. A strict search was made in ditches and pools of water near the house, fearing that the child might have fallen in the water. During the search, a heap of dung near the house was observed that had been newly turned up. There they found the body of the child mangled in a horrible condition. The boy, who was the only person capable of committing the murder, still denied his part in it. A coroner's jury met and the boy was again charged. He persisted in denying the crime. At length, he fell to crying and said he would tell the whole truth. He confessed that he carried the girl to the dung heap. He cut her body with a large knife that he found about the house and he buried her. The boy repeated the confession before a neighboring justice and added to the facts at further trials that "it was the devil who put him upon committing the act." The authorities felt great concern about the cruelty of taking the life of a boy ten years old, yet they felt the example of this boy's punishment might be a means of deterring children from like offenses. Sparing this boy merely because of his age was considered contrary to justice and to the public welfare. The sentence should be allowed to take its course unless "there remaineth any doubt touching his guilt." All the judges involved concurred in this principle, but several of them felt tenderness and caution, and they advised the chief justice to send another reprieve. After several reprieves the chief justice determined to send no more and to leave the prisoner to the justice of the law. But before a period of nine years after the time of the murder, in the year 1757, His Majesty granted pardon to the boy on the condition that he enter the sea service. A full account of this case is found in the *Gentlemen's Magazine,* volume XVIII (May 1748), page 235. An interesting note by the editor of this magazine is found at the end of the article: "Judge Hales ordered a boy of the same age to be hanged who burned a child in a cradle."

A report that illustrates a child's responsibility for knowledge of right and wrong follows:

One ten-year-old was hanged for killing companions while a nine-year-old who was involved in the same case was not sentenced to death. The reasoning for this was that the nine-year-old boy hid himself while the other hid the body he had killed. The latter manifested a consciousness of guilt and a discretion between good and evil.

The attitude that sparing young people merely because

of their tender years might be of dangerous consequence to the public appears again and again. People of that time feared spreading a notion that children might commit atrocious crimes with impunity. Judges, in some cases, agreed that young children were proper subjects for capital punishment if there was strong and clear evidence that they were guilty.

But as long ago as the eighteenth century, there were people who expressed great concern about the effect of jail (or gaol) confinement on children. William Smith reports in the *State of the Gaols in London, Westminster, and Borough of Southwark (London 1776)* that "to suffer children to remain in a gaol is very impolitic for many reasons; besides crowding the house unreasonably, it not only corrupts their morals but injures their health, stops their growth, hurts their looks, and endangers their lives. . . ."

One of the more common methods of punishing or sentencing delinquent children in England during the late eighteenth century and early nineteenth century was transportation to Australia. The method of transportation to Australia was far from pleasant by today's standards or even by standards of that day. Children were kept in county jails for a given portion of time, varying from three months to several years. They were then put on board hulks (boats) designed for this purpose. On the way to the docks, some were chained to the tops of coaches and others traveled in open caravans exposed to rain or any other form of weather. They were watched, taunted, and mocked by people along the way. Children were fettered together with older men and paraded through the kingdom in a cruel manner. It was noted by a sympathetic observer that several children were heavily fettered, ragged, and sickly on the way to the hulks.

In one account of transported convicts under the age of

twenty-one years, there were five who were referred to as infants of eleven, seven children who were age twelve, seventeen children age thirteen, thirty-two boys and girls age fourteen, and sixty-five of fifteen years of age.

A number of attempts were made by various societies who considered themselves to be charitable to help children who had committed offenses. An outstanding example was the Philanthropic Society, which was begun in London in 1788 for the prevention of crimes, caring for the offsprings of convicts, and caring for other destitute and delinquent children. Its object was reported to unite "the spirit of charity with the principles of trade, and to erect a temple of philanthropy on the foundations of virtuous industry. . . ." These wards of society for whom they cared were to be employed primarily in the production of such things as they consumed. According to the plan, a small number of children were housed under the supervision of a matron and were employed in knitting stockings and weaving lace and garters. The number of buildings that housed the children increased gradually. At one point in time, boys and girls were separated, and at first, the boys found difficulty with meal preparation. Trades such as shoemaking, tailoring, knitting, and spinning were taught, and agriculture, which was considered "man's natural labor and the primary spring of riches of health and happiness" was encouraged. The mode of living in houses as separate families appears to be an early illustration of the present cottage system that is used to help house foster children of today. Wards of the Philanthropic Society were considered to have been rescued from a life in which they would be "pests and annoyers of society and heirs of misery or victims to the law."

It is interesting to note a few of the descriptions of the children who were under the care of the society. Two boys

were received with the note that their father was now under a
sentence of death in Newgate Prison. Their mother was
living on Carrier Street, a place where few but those of the
most abandoned character resided. There is no note that the
children had committed any crime.

A girl, age five, was the daughter of a prisoner in
Newgate. A young boy was on record as being the son of a
convict on board the hulk *Woolrich* and his mother a
vagrant woman. A thirteen-year-old girl who was deserted
by her father and mother was found begging about the
streets and selling matches. The Philanthropic Society
aimed to help these children by removing them from evil
company where they "were destined to ruin and to educate
and instruct them in some useful trade or occupation." By
the time the Reform, as it was then called, had received as
many as ninety children, there were among them several
who had been rescued from "retreats of villany [sic] and
haunts of prostitution."

By 1804 the Philanthropic Society had admitted five
boys who were under sentence of death, and a number of
other offenders had been admitted. In one case a ten-year-
old boy who had only stolen a watch had been put under the
care of this society. Although the Reform may have helped
only a comparatively small number of children, it was
indeed superior in quality to the majority of situations that
befell children who either broke the law or who had no place
to go other than an almshouse or prison.

About five hundred children were confined in Newgate
Prison in London between 1813 and 1817 where they were
mixed with the general prison system. The conditions there
were such that the keeper not only did not consider the
morals of the children but also "took no care of the sick until
he got a warning to perform a funeral." Some of the children

who were committed to Newgate Prison had done nothing more than steal a loaf of bread to keep from starving. The sentence for the same offense committed by others just consisted of flogging and discharge after being placed in a temporary refuge for several months. (Hardly an example of equality of justice.)

Although in olden days children were generally regarded as just another worker for the family or wards of the state, many thoughtful individuals were expressing concern about what was happening to young people who committed offenses. In addition to the jailing of children in cruel ways, punishments seemed so uneven that some members of a community took some action against the situation.

The first report from the committee of the Society for the Improvement of Prison Discipline and for the Reformation of Juvenile Offenders appeared in London in 1818. Those members of the committee who interviewed young offenders were very alarmed at the increase in juvenile delinquency in London. They considered "the neglect of prison discipline was one cause of more crime and misery." They decided to make the consideration of prison discipline a primary object of their association, so the name of the committee was changed to that of the Society for the Improvement of Prison Discipline and for the Reformation of Juvenile Offenders.

In one case that was investigated, an eight-year-old girl was found in confinement in one of the prisons in the city of London. She had been committed for a month on a charge of child stealing. The report of the Society for the Improvement of Prison Discipline notes that the parents had driven the girl into the streets to beg, sell matches, and sing ballads. When she returned home without money, she was severely beaten and would have been turned out into the streets helpless and destitute if it had not been for visitors who placed her in a temporary refuge.

While reports from the committee of the Society for the Improvement of Prison Discipline and Reformation of Juvenile Offenders were issued annually for a number of years and occasionally after that, they were *generally* overlooked. The society became more interested in general prison reform than in reclaiming the juvenile delinquents, even though their intentions seemed good.

Other attempts at changing the treatment of children were made without much success both in England and in the United States. Until 1899, treatment of juvenile offenders in the United States followed the same tradition as that of England. In 1832, there was a movement in both countries to move the children out of the prisons. Helping to get children away from hardened criminals and to reduce periods of confinement was indeed progress.

While reformers in England were involved with the Philanthropic Society, people in the United States began shifting some of the emphasis from trying to reform hardened adult offenders to the prevention of crime by the means of reformation of juvenile delinquents. The first institution for juvenile delinquents in the United States was the New York House of Refuge, which came about largely through the work of two men. One of these men, James W. Gerard, was a young lawyer who had defended a fourteen-year-old boy accused of stealing a bird. Gerard won an acquittal for the boy by arguing that prison would corrupt him. The young lawyer was so interested in this case that he began to investigate prison facilities for juveniles in New York. He decided to join a society that was interested in the reformation of juvenile delinquents. The other man, Isaac Collins, was a Quaker who was already a member of this same society, namely the Society for the Prevention of

Pauperism. Collins was preparing a report for the 1822 meeting of the society on ways of carrying out its noble purposes. With the help of Gerard, the report led to the creation of the first separate institution for juvenile delinquents, the New York House of Refuge mentioned above. At the time of its opening, society considered a juvenile delinquent as any young person who had broken the law or wandered about the streets, neither in school nor at work, and who obviously lacked "good family." The inference that anyone who was not in school or at work was delinquent is indeed clear.

From its small beginning, the House of Refuge grew and changed in character. After several years, the rules prescribed continuous activity for the inmates during their waking hours, except for some time on Sundays. Punishments for lack of industriousness or disobeying other rules included being sent to bed without supper. In more serious cases, a boy or girl might be made to drink an herb tea that caused profuse sweating. Solitary confinements and the use of binding in iron fetters are reported for severe offenses. But in spite of all this, there are reports that there was some progressive philosophy at the New York House of Refuge. One aspect of this progressive philosophy was the practice of "binding out" children in foster homes.

Similar institutions to the New York House of Refuge were established in several other cities within a few years of its beginnings. There was also considerable exchange of ideas between the New York authorities and the Philanthropic Society in England. Additional efforts in reform resulted in the establishment of state-supported institutions for juvenile delinquents.

By 1855, the first American institution for young offenders based entirely on the "family system" was established in Massachusetts. The Children's Aid Society and other groups that pioneered in a system of placing juvenile delinquents in family situations made an important step forward.

While earlier reformers had placed great faith in the power of education to remedy social evils, they neglected the significance of the family in teaching moral values. Unfortunately, there were inadequate screening systems in selecting the families to receive children in these early foster care situations and much of it had to be abandoned. In some cases children were sent from one state to another and this led to the passage of laws prohibiting the placement of "incorrigible, insane, criminal, or diseased children" within their boundaries.

Although America's chidren had begun to come into focus as individuals, there were many problems that arose. For example, the use of methods that worked with an emotionally adjusted child did not always work with a juvenile delinquent. The needed understanding of behavior and motivation did not come until later years.

Many responsible citizens made contributions to the improvement of conditions for juvenile offenders during the last half of the nineteenth century. One of the most outstanding was Jane Addams, who has been called America's first social worker. She founded the famous Hull House in Chicago's ghetto where troubled children were offered help and understanding. Settlement houses here and there throughout the United States played an important part in the prevention of juvenile delinquency. Conditions, however, at the turn of the century were still unusually cruel for the young person who was sentenced for a crime.

About the year 1900, there were sixty-five reformatories for juveniles in the United States. According to the superintendent of the reform school in Plainfield, Indiana,

T.J. Charlton, "The rapid growth of the juvenile reformatories in the United States is marvelous when we consider that it has all taken place in the last 50 years."

The reformatories were based on one of two systems, the "cottage system" or one in which all inmates were placed in a single building where an official had charge of a large number of children. About the year 1900, there was much disagreement about which system was better, although some felt they now had solved the problem. According to Mr. Charlton, "It was found that when delinquent children were given an industrial education they were more easily reformed."* The best estimate of the successs of juvenile reformatories gave the rate of 80 to 90 percent. An interesting comment in the same Charlton report follows: "Boys are not reformed in a day. The average time of detention in the juvenile reformatories of this country is about 2 years, and we cannot over-estimate of so preparing them that their hands and hearts may be stronger in all those higher virtues that ennoble and adorn human character." It appears that Mr. Charlton felt that the reformatory system of the United States was solving most of its delinquent problems. Not surprisingly, many felt otherwise.

Certainly, Jane Addams looked at the problem through different eyes. Her approach was a desire to help young people rather than punish them. She noted that, in Chicago, boys found themselves branded as delinquents as a result of their pursuit of excitement, and that for the great majority of young offenders, there were no specialized places. When the police caught a young person violating the law, they treated

---

*T.J. Charlton, *The Reformatory System in the United States,* House of Representatives Document 459, Fifty-sixth Congress, First Session, Washington, D.C. 1900.

him or her as they would an adult. The offender was taken to
police courts where a magistrate set bail. If the person could
not provide bail money, he or she was sent to a jail cell in the
police station to await trial. At the trial, police justices
frequently either assessed a small fine or sent the offender to
the city house of correction for a brief period of imprison-
ment. Often, because of the child's age, he or she might be
sent home. In serious offenses, cases usually were sent to the
grand jury for indictment, just as in the case of an adult. Jane
Addams and others recognized that treating juveniles as
adults did not work.

In Chicago's Cook County Jail, it is reported that about
fifteen cases involving children were sent to the grand jury
each month. Most offenses were petty, such as stealing
pigeons or rabbits from barns, or hoodlum acts that in the
country would be considered boyish acts rather than crime,
so the grand jury refused to indict about 75 percent of the
cases that it heard. This system had the effect of bringing
young people at the police station in contact with adult
criminals. It also gave children the idea that they could
commit offenses without prosecution since they would
probably escape because of their youth. This is still one of
the criticisms of today's juvenile court.

Even at the end of the nineteenth century, there was a
certain amount of political involvement and some youths
were freed as political favors to parents. It is estimated that
about one third of the boys sent to prison secured pardons.
About this time, the Chicago Women's Club agitated for a
separate court for children and pushed their cause over a
period of years. With a number of allies, they succeeded in
influencing politicians to bring a bill to the Illinois legisla-
ture. Action on this finally resulted in the Juvenile Court
Act, which became law on July 1, 1899. Under this new law,
the treatment and control of dependent, neglected, and

delinquent children were under the broad powers of the juvenile court. This court could place the children in institutions or with individuals who could take the place of unsuitable family homes. The court became the guardian or the responsible parent of the child. This concept of the state as parent was actually introduced in America in 1636 when a young boy of Plymouth Colony was indentured by the state and was given to a widow to keep as a foster child. In England, during the late fourteenth and early fifteenth centuries, the King's Court of Chancery had the power of guardianship over the children who were abandoned or willfully neglected by their parents. In 1899, in Cook County, Chicago, Illinois, the child *who had offended the law ceased to be a criminal* and had the status of a child who needed care, protection, and discipline. All this was to be directed toward rehabilitation. At this point in time, offenders became wards of the state and the emphasis was on treatment rather than on punishment.

The Juvenile Court of Cook County was widely imitated throughout the United States. Within a generation, practically every state had enacted statutes establishing juvenile courts or their equivalent. Although the juvenile court was the culmination of a long-term trend, it did not reach all states in the United States immediately. Juvenile courts of various types eventually reached all states, with the last enacting the necessary legislation in 1945. Now there was a new kind of machinery outside the criminal law for handling young offenders. According to many authorities, this, in the legal sense, created the term "delinquent child."

Although the introduction of juvenile courts seemed a great step forward from courts where children were taken into custody in the manner of adults, there is much concern about the juvenile courts of today. The "kindly parent, the state" is an expression that is sometimes used sarcastically.

3

WHO IS A JUVENILE DELINQUENT?

Defining "juvenile delinquent" is so difficult that even the experts disagree. Here, using actual cases, is one approach to answering the question, Who is a juvenile delinquent?

Robert is a seventeen-year-old boy who lived in rural Indiana. He was charged with drinking, with being incorrigible, and with possessing liquor in a car parked in front of a local lodge. Robert was sent to the Boy's Training School for these offenses and was now classed as a juvenile delinquent. If he was not already headed for a life of crime, he well might be after he associates with other delinquents at the training center.

Bill is a fifteen-year-old boy who hitchhiked to Florida for his spring vacation from school. He spent all his money there and had no way of returning home quickly when he had word that there was an emergency in his family. He spotted a car with keys in it, drove it home to the northern state in which he lived, and took the car to the police station after he reached home. The owner of the car, although upset, decided not to prosecute, and the local police did not bring the case to trial. Bill was warned that this kind of behavior could lead to trouble, and the episode was soon forgotten. Bill was never labeled as a juvenile delinquent.

Although he is not quite eighteen years old, Lee has already been sent to the local training school for the second time. The first time he was committed after a long police record, which included assault and battery, first-degree burglary, missing person, bicycle theft, and fifteen false fire alarms. The false alarms were part of a burglary scheme when Lee was a member of a gang who robbed the garages of homes after setting false fire alarms and turning the attention of owners to a possible fire. After five months of incarceration for first-degree burglary, Lee was paroled. But after four months, he was arrested for assault and battery and carrying a deadly weapon. There is little question that Lee fits the definition of a juvenile delinquent.

Ernest lived in a ghetto in Chicago where he was being intimidated into joining a gang of blacks who were involved in street conflicts. Ernest's parents moved to a rural white community in northern Indiana where his family felt he would find better company. But the black family was not accepted there and before long Ernest was on indefinite probation, having been picked up for trespassing. About three weeks after being arrested, Ernest was found to have violated the terms of his probation by "using obscene language on the school bus, changing seats on the school bus, and getting off the bus to smoke at short stops." He was committed to the Indiana Boy's School as a juvenile delinquent.

Sue is a fifteen-year-old girl who was committed to training school for "using intoxicating beverages, violating curfew, and being truant from school." Police found her in a car in a parking lot with a can of beer. Upon questioning, she answered in a way the police considered "smart-alecky." This episode brought questioning at the police station, followed by release in the custody of her parents until the court appearance two weeks later. At this time, the judge was advised that she had been truant from school and that she did not appear to be a good subject for probation. Since it was claimed that Sue needed close supervision, she was committed to a youth development center. Here she did superior school work and caused no behavior problem. Was she a juvenile delinquent? Might she have solved her problems within the community and made a better adjustment there?

Betty at age fourteen had no place to live since her family was unable to provide an adequate home. Her mother was considered mentally incompetent and her father was in and out of prison. A foster family took care of her for a while after the state placed her in their home, but they were very conservative and restrictive. In school, Betty lied about her status as a "welfare child" and would go without lunch rather than reveal the truth. Then she began stealing small items. This kind of behavior could not be tolerated by the foster parents. Since no other resources were available, Betty was committed to the state training school. She was a child who could not go home. By some definitions, she is a juvenile delinquent.

A number of studies show that about half the girls in training schools have committed no crime other than running away from home. In some cases, their running away is a plea for help, help that is not usually supplied by the training schools. Many boys and girls are taken to juvenile court by parents who have "lost control" and who hope that their children will find help in a confined situation. Many other parents take children to juvenile court because they are not wanted at home.

One case reported to Congress during an investigation of juvenile delinquency tells of the plight of a child in Illinois named Vicki. Her father was incarcerated on a murder charge three months before Vicki was born. Her mother tried to raise Vicki but the girl had emotional problems. Tests showed that her IQ was very high. It was felt that one of the reasons for not getting along in school was that she was brilliant and bored. When the girl was nine years old, a number of people suggested that the mother admit to the court that she had neglected Vicki so she could place the child in a state institution. "You just have to admit you have neglected her and cannot handle her anymore, and the state will take over the raising of the child. They will put her in a nice boarding school." Actually, the mother followed this advice and the state did become the guardian, placing the girl in an orphanage. But after three months, the staff at the orphanage claimed that they did not have the personnel to adequately care for Vicki and she was placed in an institution known as the Audy Home. This is a maximum security institution for pretrial detention of delinquent children. At the time of Vicki's placement, a mixture of neglected, mentally retarded, and emotionally disturbed children as well as delinquents were in the institution.

While Vicki was at the Audy Home, her stay was turbulent. She had many emotional problems and needed professional help, but so far she had not shown any delinquent tendencies. However, she was considered "high strung" and she did strike a matron at the home. For this, she was placed in restraint. Other episodes followed during the next eight or nine months with many severe punishments. Then Vicki went to a mental hospital. Later she was sent to the state training school for girls, when she was fourteen years old.

Here is a case of a child whose mother admitted to neglect in order to get help, but the child became a delinquent through a series of events over which she had no control. This case came to the attention of the chief attorney of the state of Illinois who filed a petition against institutions that had mistreated her by solitary confinement and restrictions and that had not looked to her future. Not many children are noticed by such an advocate.

Parents who feel that their children are juvenile delinquents sometimes change their minds when they discover what happens to boys and girls after they are committed. Under many juvenile codes today, parents alone cannot file "beyond control" petitions. Social agencies that have been working with a family try to help the child and the parents to prevent separation. When there is true neglect or abuse, the court can step in as guardian. When there are serious emotional disturbances, a child can be sent to a medical facility. But not all states have family courts, and even those states that do, have cases where the system does not work perfectly. Many children who are not juvenile delinquents at the outset become delinquent after spending some time in an institution or even in a foster home situation that is not suitable. And in some cases, there are children who seem to be headed for crime no matter how much help is available. The question, Who is a juvenile delinquent? is certainly a difficult and perhaps an impossible one to answer, but attempting to know "who" helps one to understand some of the problems of justice and injustice.

While case studies are one approach to answering the question, Who is a juvenile delinquent? another is attempting to define "juvenile delinquent." A person within a certain age group who commits acts that would be a crime if committed by an adult is one definition. The meaning of *delinquency* is relative and varies with time and place. The age group varies, too, from state to state. There is some confusion about whether it is better to raise or lower the juvenile age limit. Lowering it permits a larger number of serious offenders to be tried like adults and be given adult penalties.

In most states, the juvenile courts have jurisdiction over offenders between the ages of seven and eighteen. The state is to be the kindly parent who is supposed to act "in the best interests of the child" when a child breaks the law of his or her state. In many cases, the laws that are broken are laws that apply only to young people. For example, an adult can run away, stay away from school, and has no curfew. An adult cannot be committed on the basis of a parent's, neighbor's, or school's claim that his or her behavior is incorrigible. Children who break such laws are called status offenders, and in some states these children are also labeled with terms such as Persons in Need of Supervision or Child in Need of Services (PINS and CHINS).

Some states are moving in the direction of changing runaway laws, but one change often affects other situations. For example, in Indiana, a bill that removed runaways from the jurisdiction of juvenile courts and the police was passed under the title S.B. 90. Some confusion resulted partly because the law was interpreted locally with different responses.

In some cases, authorities looked for other offenses and found they could hold runaways on the charge of stolen bicycles, and so forth. Not every one felt running away should be legalized. In addition to this, when the law was changed there were not enough provisions made for those who now legally ran away from home. Because the runaways were underage, they were not given the right to work, seek treatment, or other rights needed by a person to live independently. So, while the courts could not classify runaways as delinquents, they could not provide any services for them because they were removed from the court system. (The National Runaway Youth Act helps fund some programs for runaways who do not reach the court.) One of the lessons that other states may learn from these problems in Indiana is that the whole legislative area of youth's rights is a complex one, and sometimes new problems are created when an old one is corrected.

Is a juvenile delinquent a person who commits an unlawful act, one who *has been caught* committing an unlawful act, or one who is punished for committing an unlawful act? Many young people who engage in activities that are minor infractions of the law are not caught, and many are not punished. Of these, only a fraction become repeaters. For many, financial and social status are a determining factor.

Consider the following rather typical case. Two boys are playing football in an area of the park where such activity is forbidden. They are warned by the police that their actions could lead to arrest. The boys stop for a while, grumble about the situation and the police, then smoke marijuana in the nearby woods. The same policemen find them and take them to the police station where they will be held until parents are notified. One boy's parents are at work and cannot be reached. The other boy's parents come immediately to the police station and promise to punish the boy. He is released in their custody. The boy without help goes through a long series of events beyond his control: He appears in juvenile court and is sentenced to incarceration where he is exposed to juveniles who have committed many violent offenses. This boy learns from them and during the following few years returns to juvenile court on many occasions. The difference for these boys was primarily a case of parents who cared. Sometimes it is a matter of money for lawyers, knowledge of the law, or the attitude of authorities.

With the introduction of the juvenile justice system, the definition of a delinquent child was made to include more than violaters of the criminal code, and the emphasis became treatment, not punishment.

Since the juvenile delinquent had now become the neglected, the abused, the runaway, and anyone in need of help, the court was charged with a tremendous task. Some authorities criticize the effort as too grand. In expecting too much, the result has been the treatment of many young criminals no differently, and in many cases less harshly, than the neglected and dependent child. Certainly, those who created the juvenile court had no conception of the complexities in its future.

Perhaps juvenile delinquency cannot be defined or prevented. But many authorities feel that the separation of status offenders from the violent offenders who repeat and are released again and again after a short punishment may help to determine who is really a juvenile delinquent. How can such a person best be helped and society best be protected?

4

WANDERERS, WASTRELS, MUGGERS, AND OTHERS IN JUVENILE COURT

Who comes to juvenile court? Some of those who are typical of the less violent offenders were described in the last chapter. Certainly a wide variety of young people appear in juvenile courts before the judges who will play such a large part in their futures. According to some estimates, one child in nine can be expected to appear in juvenile court before the age of eighteen.

Society's attitude of responsibility to these children varies from "Society needs protection" to "It is society's responsibility to remedy the inequities that produce such children." When one listens to a case where the whole picture of the child's problems are shown, the "bleeding heart" tends to dominate. When one considers the damage to persons and properties by juveniles, attitudes often change.

Across the nation people are concerned about the increase in violent crimes. However, some crime reports indicate that the number of nonviolent crimes appears to be lower. Even though juvenile delinquents are not "taking over the world," as some people think, there is a great need to improve the functioning of the juvenile justice system.

Edward M. Davis, former President of the International Association of Chiefs of Police, issued the following warning: ". . . as the juvenile justice system continues to operate under present constraints, we know that it is building an army of criminals who will prey on our communities. The benign neglect that we have shown has made children with special problems into monsters that will be with us forever. If improvement to this system does not come, it will insure a generation of criminals who will make the current batch look like kids at a Sunday School picnic."

There are many different reasons for coming to juvenile court. There are those who commit offenses such as murders; forcible rape; robbery; aggravated assault; breaking and entering; larceny-theft; auto theft; arson; forgery and counterfeiting; fraud; embezzlement; buying, receiving, and possessing stolen property; vandalism; possessing or carrying weapons; prostitution; narcotic possession and other drug offenses; gambling; offenses against family and children; driving under the influence; curfew; vagrancy; and disorderly conduct.

There is no general consistency of laws dealing with juvenile offenders, or neglected, abused, and abandoned children in the United States. Often the plight of the juvenile offender who is protected by "the kindly parent, the state" is one in which everyone but the child has a voice. How did this well-meaning intent to reform, which brought the juvenile court into being in the first place, turn into a tyranny of reform? How did the state gain so much authority over dependent children? Much has happened to the juvenile court system since the days of its origin, both in the number of people involved and in the way it does or does not carry out the original philosophy of its function. Today, punishment is being recommended for violent crimes. This replaces the state's acting as the loving parent and protector until the child is rehabilitated or reaches his or her twenty-first birthday.

While may people have agreed that there is something wrong with the present juvenile justice system, few feel that they have the answers for making it right. According to one report, the juvenile justice system works most efficiently when it deals with a young person who has committed a serious offense. If there is proof of guilt beyond a reasonable doubt, the child is either placed on probation or sent to a state training school unless transferred to adult criminal court. The time spent in custody may depend partly on the sentence and partly on the family's interests and resources. Critics contend that there is "one court for the rich and one court for the poor" and numerous studies show that there is different handling of offenders, based on neighborhood and economic circumstances.

Over one million young people appear in juvenile courts each year, and each case is different. Behind each hearing is an individual story. In some cases, the child may, theoretically, be incarcerated until his or her twenty-first birthday; the child who comes from a family that will cooperate may be released in six months. Thus the neglected or abused child whose parents do not show interest may well spend a longer time for a minor offense than the violent offender whose parents come to the rescue.

What happens to a child who breaks the law also depends partly on where he or she lives. Juvenile justice or injustice is a local matter, with about three thousand juvenile courts in the United States.

Part of the problem in the present system of juvenile courts is overcrowding. When family court in New York, for example, sends one hundred cases into the system each month for placement in an institution, one hundred children must be released in order to free beds for the new cases even though the staff believes some of the releases are not wise.

Many problems that could be redefined as welfare, educational, or family problems find their way to juvenile court because children are considered predelinquent. Their diversion would help to relieve the overburdened courts and allow judges to concentrate on those who commit serious offenses.

Certainly the juvenile court system is in need of some major reform. When one attorney began searching for ways to improve the juvenile justice system, he compared the situation to picking up a flat, damp rock and seeing a lot of bugs and worms under it. The initial response is to put down the rock and walk away. Fortunately, many people continue to explore the problem of juvenile justice and injustice and are attempting to help those who are being hurt. Looking at the overall effect, all of society is being hurt by children who come out of training schools and other confined situations as muggers, rapists, and murderers.

Should the juvenile justice system "mollycoddle those wise little punks?" The Honorable Edward V. Healey, Jr., Associate Justice of the Rhode Island Family Court, says that he once echoed the sentiments that a "heavy hand" and a "little time in the lock-up" would solve all the problems. He was filled with fire and brimstone until he worked with these people for a while. Now he calls the above a simplistic approach to a complex problem.

Many judges who move on to other courts, such as adult criminal court, retain an interest in the problems of juvenile justice and injustice. One of these people is Associate Justice David Zenoff of the Supreme Court of Nevada. He sent the following opinion to the United States Senate to help with the investigation of juvenile delinquency:

> *In one area alone we find that care and treatment at the outset might well reduce at least the incidents of young people involved in murder. That area is what we call delinquent mental defectives. I'm informed that in three cases entertained by the Nevada Supreme Court alone within the period of 30 days three murders were committed for nickels and dimes against three innocent unsuspecting victims, a cab driver, a store owner, and a cigarette salesman, all unrelated to each other, all committed separately by three different 17-year-old boys and the common denominator was that in their very early childhood they were seriously mentally retarded and their conditions went untreated and uncared for.*

Over three thousand juvenile court judges in the United States are committed to fulfilling the promise of the juvenile court. Each has his or her own theory on how to help delinquents, and each may try to accord every child brought before him or her with individual, understanding care. Each judge may dispose of every case in the way that follows his philosophy of the juvenile court if he has access to facilities that carry out the plans. All the information that is presented is confidential and such information is sealed from the public and from use against the child after adult age is reached. But this privileged, confidential, and supposedly

perceptive inquiry into the whole child which is brought
before the judge is often far from realistic. Sometimes,
rather than be guided away from a life of crime by a kindly
judge, a child is committed to one.

A good juvenile court judge is expected to appear
tough, be a good disciplinarian. At the same time the judge is
to show sincere concern for helping the child before the
bench and to treat the child with respect, dignity, and
understanding. For many children who appear in juvenile
court, a stern lecture from the judge and some guidance
from a probation officer who replaces an authority figure
missing in the home appears to work. About one half of the
cases received by juvenile court are thus dismissed. But not
all children are psychologically equipped to profit from such
a confrontation. Many return to the environment that
caused their problems only to see the system as a joke
because they run little risk of punishment.

Many citizens heap blame on the judges who must
make the decisions in juvenile court. Not only are the cases
and courts at wide variance in different localities, but also
the case load of the judges varies. In many communities the
same judge sits for criminal court as for juvenile court. Such
a judge might spend most of the day with a very serious adult
case and squeeze in the case of a child who has been brought
to the attention of authorities for spraying paint on a town
memorial. The judge may be interrupted during the juvenile
case for an emergency in adult criminal court. Can such a
situation give a judge the fair psychological approach to the
child's case? A child and his parents who have been waiting
for two or more weeks for a case to come to the hearing
might find it lasts only five minutes. And what happens in
that five minutes may play a very large part in the lives of a
number of people.

A juvenile court judge is charged with several functions. Achieving a balance among them can be difficult even if one has considerable time. Imagine trying to satisfy the following charges:

1. to protect the community

2. to act in the best interest and welfare of the child

3. to uphold the dignity of the law and the public's faith in the judicial system

In many cases, the judge belongs to a "different world" from that of the child who comes before him or her. The judge must try to empathize with an environment that is unfamiliar. Many people who work in the field of juvenile justice complain that the judge imposes his or her own particular brand of culture and morals on those who come before the court. In most cases in the past, and some in the present, no one speaks for the child. This is true in spite of a landmark decision in juvenile justice that should have changed this. Although the Gault Decision is not new, many children still are not represented by lawyers.

The Gault Decision followed what happened to a fifteen-year-old boy in Arizona, Gerald Gault. On June 8, 1964, Gerald and another boy were taken into custody after a neighbor complained that she had received a lewd and indecent phone call. Both of Gerald's parents were at work that morning, and the police left no notice of his arrest. When his parents returned home they did not know what had happened to Gerald, so they sent his older brother out to search for him. The older brother discovered that Gerald was at the Children's Detention Home. He and the mother went there, were told "why Jerry was there" and that a hearing was set for the following day. Since Gerald's father was at work, the mother and brother appeared at the hearing along with probation officers. No formal or informal record of the hearing was made, but Gerald was questioned about the telephone call and released a few days later pending further hearings. Since no records were made, accounts of exactly what happened in the court on the ninth of June varied when discussed on future dates. According to one report, Gerald admitted to making one of the indecent remarks. His mother remembered only that he admitted dialing the neighbor's phone number.

A second hearing was held for Gerald Gault before the same judge on June 15, at which time Mrs. Gault requested that the neighbor be present. Mrs. Gault was told that this was not necessary, and the neighbor was not called to appear. At the end of the hearing, Gerald was committed to the state industrial school as a juvenile delinquent for the period of his minority unless sooner discharged by process of law. Since Gerald was fifteen years old at the time of the hearing, this sentence could have meant a period of six years.

The judge, when questioned, gave various reasons for the severity of this decision. One was that Gerald Gault was a delinquent child since he had "stolen a baseball glove" two years previous and had lied to the police department about it. The judge also testified that Gerald had violated a part of the Arizona Criminal Code, which states that a person who uses vulgar, abusive, or obscene language in the presence of a woman or child is guilty of a misdemeanor. If an adult breaks this same law and is convicted, the penalty is a fine ranging from five to fifty dollars or two months in prison.

Since no appeal was permitted in juvenile cases under

juvenile law, Gerald's lawyer filed a writ of habeas corpus (a document requiring that a person be brought before a court or judge) with the Supreme Court of Arizona. After considerable legal processes, the case reached the United States Supreme Court. The famous Gault Decision was handed down from the United States Supreme Court on May 16, 1967. Among other things, it held that Gerald Gault was deprived of due process of law by being denied adequate notice, record of the proceedings, and right to counsel. This landmark decision was the basis on which broad reform in all juvenile courts could be founded. The Supreme Court of the United States concluded that juveniles, like adults, are entitled to the following Bill of Rights safeguards:

A notice of the charge placed against the offender

The right to legal counsel

The right to confront and cross-examine complaintants and other witnesses

The privilege of remaining silent, and other protection against self-incrimination

The Gault Decision had a significant impact on juvenile court proceedings throughout the United States; only part of the aspects are mentioned above. But in spite of this and other progress,* it is obvious that all does not function smoothly in a great many juvenile courts.

---

*Kent Decision (1966). Before a juvenile case can be shifted to criminal court, a hearing must be held in which the juvenile is entitled to counsel. Winship Decision (1970). When juveniles are charged with an offense that would be a crime for an adult, charges must be proved beyond a reasonable doubt.

Between 1966 and 1971, a number of rulings besides the Gault Decision tested the constitutionality of the routine procedures of the juvenile court and helped to a degree in the reassessment of the founding premises. By 1977 the implementation of some of these movements that guarantee children's rights had not reached many of those who appeared in juvenile court. In the *San Diego Law Review*, A. Bruce Ferguson and Alan C. Douglas reported that 96 percent of the children they studied failed to understand their rights and voluntarily waived them.

While there is no typical juvenile court scene, the hearings consist of two parts. If the first part, the fact-finding phase, determines that the young person is delinquent, a dispositional hearing follows. At this, the judge is charged with concentrating on the best interests of the child while at the same time affording protection to the community. If each child is to be considered as an individual, there must be ample time to explore all aspects of the case. Even with the minimum of time for a case, there are backlogs. Lack of time is such a problem in certain courts that the backlog of cases is over four thousand.

In May of 1976, a judge of the New York City Family Court submitted his letter of resignation to the mayor. In his letter,* the Honorable Simeon Golar describes some of the reasons why he feels he cannot continue to serve in this capacity.

In recent months sitting in an Intake Part in Queens, I have on many days heard more than 125 cases—with an average of less than three

*© 1976 by *The New York Times Company*. Reprinted by permission.

minutes per case! Certainly a judge needs more
time than a moment or two to decide whether
to take away a mother's child or to have a man
arrested or imprisoned for nonsupport, or to
remand someone for psychiatric examination.
And certainly those who appear before the court
and the entire public are entitled to better than
this.

In his letter of resignation, Judge Golar describes what he considers to be the family court's greatest failing: the area of juvenile delinquency. He believes the juvenile court system was flawed from its beginning at the turn of the century because it was based on the notion that all antisocial behavior engaged in by children is pathological (caused by or involving disease) and is treatable. At the time of his resignation, delinquents could be released in a month or two from the state training school no matter how serious the offending act. A boy who committed armed robbery or a boy who defaced a subway car might both be considered juvenile delinquents. Each might be released within the same period of time. Such treatment provides a token punishment for juvenile delinquents that offers neither hope nor effective rehabilitation according to Judge Golar.

Certainly Judge Golar is not alone in his plea for a better system of juvenile justice. Reform is the concern of many groups who see the need to minimize the number of juveniles placed in confinement. The "child saver" rationale that has brought about institutionalization for many has been the subject of much reassessment. Attention is being focused on the role of the juvenile court and the importance of separating the young who seriously threaten public safety from the boys and girls who are homeless or who are having problems such as truancy and other status offenses.

Concern and hard work brought about the Juvenile Justice and Delinquency Prevention Act of 1974. This act is designed to make prevention of juvenile crime a national priority. One purpose of the act is to prevent young people from becoming entangled in a juvenile justice system that has failed. It assists state and local governments, as well as individual and private organizations, in developing more sensible, less costly, and ultimately more productive assistance for young people who are already in the system. A major objective of the Juvenile Justice Act is to prevent youth facilities from continuing to be nurseries for crime. It forbids the incarceration of status offenders and requires the separation of juveniles from adult offenders. Those states that do not comply with these requirements are not eligible for the same funding as those that do. The findings and declaration of purpose of the Juvenile Justice and Delinquency Prevention Act of 1974 are listed in the appendix of this book.

The passage of the Act was not a magic wand or panacea for the problems in the juvenile justice system. But some states did move toward the goals of separating status offenders from detention with violent offenders in secure facilities and the removal of some children from adult jails. But even though some states passed laws prohibiting the incarceration of status offenders, others continued to put them in state training schools.

Bess was one of the fairly typical status offenders and one of the more fortunate. She ran away from home and was brought to juvenile court because her mother filed a petition alleging that she was a runaway. When it was discovered that Bess was abused at home by her mother's live-in boyfriend, that her father was an alcoholic, and that no one really wanted her, Bess was placed in a foster home. Although she received little attention from an understaffed social welfare system, she was fortunate in being placed with a caring family. She was fortunate, too, in coming before a judge who took the time and trouble to find out about her background.

A staggering number of children are processed by the juvenile justice system each year. Many people feel that there is overprocessing. In the case of status offenders, no intervention may be as effective as, or even better than, an experience with the system. Research studies show that about 80 percent of all juveniles commit an offense or two and then stop, even if they are not arrested. However, many people accuse the police of being too lenient. Much depends on the child, the offense, the judge, and the resources of the community. There are no easy answers.

5

THE VIOLENT OFFENDER

BOY, 15 SEIZED IN KNIFE SLAYING!

**TWO JUVENILES KILL WOMAN
FOR PURSE CONTAINING $3**

TWELVE-YEAR-OLD ACCUSED OF MURDER!

These are some of the headlines that anger and frighten newspaper readers. These are headlines that prompt people to say that something is very wrong with the young people of today. Readers would be even more upset if the stories beneath the headlines revealed the many times that the violent offenders had been arrested in the past, but that information is confidential. Even so, the "revolving door syndrome," in which the violent offender is merely reprimanded and sent back out into the streets, is familiar to most people. What is not well known is that only a small percentage of young people commit serious crimes.

The delinquents who stab and shoot are part of the

vicious cycle of detention, incarceration, and crime. While the short length of their detention is being criticized, the budgets of many large cities are suffering from cutbacks in funds that are already insufficient for rehabilitating criminals. Many institutions are understaffed. There are numerous reports of boys dominating staff members, and of abuse of staff members and children who are being held in institutions.

The violent environment in many poverty areas of large cities has been called the breeding ground for crime. And violent street crime is reaching beyond the big cities. Consider the following case:

Two twelve-year-old girls were walking home from school along a bicycle path in a pleasant suburban community. Two boys appeared from behind some bushes and raped the girls on mattresses that they had thrown on the ground. Then they stabbed both girls many times and ran away. One girl, still alive, managed to walk until she reached a railroad workman, who alerted the police and called an ambulance. The boys, one aged fifteen and one aged sixteen, returned to their homes.

One boy went to school and told his friends that the boys who attacked the girls should be dealt with harshly. The other boy, a dropout, was not missed by any school system.

The girl who survived was able to help identify the two boys. They were taken into custody. In the state where this crime occurred, the sixteen-year-old could be treated like an adult. But juvenile law treated all children under the age of sixteen as unable to commit crimes. So the fifteen-year-old boy was to be free from custody when he reached the age of eighteen. The case resulted in new state legislation that was quickly enacted, but it did not affect the fifteen-year-old. It affected subsequent violent offenders as young as ten. This case was also responsible for the building of a small facility to hold youthful serious offenders.

Many people are taking another look at the young people who commit violent crimes. In some cities, the age of children who carry guns is as low as eight. A nine-year-old robbed a bank. A twelve-year-old murdered another child. In New York City, during the first six months of 1981, there were eighteen homicide arrests of children who were from seven to fifteen years of age. In the same period of time, this age group accounted for more than 2,500 arrests for robbery, serious assaults, and rape. No one knows how many crimes were committed by young people in New York and throughout the nation who were not arrested. One does know that there seems to be a wave of "kiddie crime," even though the percentage of juvenile delinquents who are causing the "kiddie crime wave" is relatively small.

Who are the violent offenders? If violent offenders are to be treated differently from other juvenile delinquents, one must arrive at a definition, and this is not easy to do. Some experts ask lawmakers to remember that each case is different, and that there cannot be a strict definition of a serious or violent juvenile offender.

Serious offenders are often defined as people who have committed crimes that have had a serious impact on the victims' lives. The public considers them to be anyone who commits a crime that "sounds" serious.

A serious juvenile offender is often defined as one whose offense history includes arrests for five or more serious offenses or one who commits one or more offenses whose severity is equal to homicide or forcible sexual intercourse. Typical serious offenses include homicide or voluntary manslaughter, forcible sexual intercourse, aggravated assault, armed robbery, burglary of an occupied residence, larceny/theft of more than one thousand dollars, auto theft without recovery of the vehicles, arson of an occupied building, kidnapping, extortion, and illegal sale of dangerous drugs.

Not everyone agrees with the above definition of a serious offender, but it is one that was developed through an assessment of the literature, statistics, and expert opinion. Some reports do not emphasize the repetition of offenses in their definitions.

Violent crime receives much attention from the media. However, it is believed that only above *five to ten percent* of those juveniles who are arrested are serious offenders. One famous study, known as the Rand report, suggests that the serious offender group makes up about 15 percent of all institutionalized delinquents in the United States, or about six thousand juveniles. Many experts believe that chronic or violent offenders commit over 50 percent of all juvenile crimes.

Some people who commit one or two serious, or even violent, crimes are not very different from their friends who pride themselves on being law-abiding citizens. According to some men and women who have had much experience with serious offenders, they are not "a breed apart" or a "different kind of person" except in cases of sociopaths or psychopaths. These latter offenders appear to have no conscience.

Consider the case of Tim. Tim "borrowed" a neighbor's car without permission when he was fourteen years old. He had never really learned to drive but he managed to speed along the highway until the car went out of control and collided head-on with an approaching vehicle. The eighteen-year-old driver of the oncoming car was killed, and a passenger was seriously injured.

In Tim's case, the judge imposed the penalty of probation and revoked his privilege of applying for a driver's license for two years beyond the time he would normally have been eligible. The judge explained his reasons for not being more severe. He did not believe that Tim, a fairly good student and usually well-behaved boy, would ever use a car unlawfully again. The judge did not believe that putting Tim in secure detention would deter any other children who were tempted to take a car. He believed Tim's act was impulsive, and that many people do things that could end in tragedy. In this case, Tim was steadily employed seven years after the incident. He was never seen in court again for another offense. What would have happened to him if the judge had sent him to a training school? Discretion, claims this judge, is what the juvenile system is all about.

Obviously, Tim does not belong to the serious offender group. Although his offense was serious, his emotional makeup was such that he felt great responsibility for the tragedy he had caused.

Fred, on the other hand, accidentally shot a man when he was fleeing from a burglary attempt at a bank. He admits that he did not lose any sleep over the incident. The man was in the wrong place at the wrong time. Fred had no concern about his own future. "If I killed the guy, tough s——. That's the way to look at it when you are young. The most you can get is a few years."

One of the great concerns in dealing with many violent offenders is their apparent lack of emotion. On the other hand, some children seem to be in a constant state of rage. If one bumps into such a boy accidentally, he may respond with the thrust of a knife. Even a smile may be taken the wrong way and provoke violent action.

Those who work in the system describe children who

yawn and fall asleep while their crimes are revealed in court. "Why worry?" they ask. "When you are young, you can be sent to youth hall, but there is a good chance you will be out in a few hours."

William was typical of the twelve- to fourteen-year-olds who form bands of street muggers, purse snatchers, and the subway thieves who terrorize city dwellers. William dropped out of school at the age of thirteen and became a mugger who preyed on old men and women. He was arrested twice, and when he was being taken by police to juvenile hall he remarked that he was only thirteen and nothing could happen to him. William was let go with a warning. Next, he beat an elderly woman in the elevator of her apartment and robbed her of three dollars. After this, a judge was more firm with him. William spent nine months in an institution, but he had only been free for a few months when he mugged an elderly man.

By the time he was nine, Tom had been arrested for burglary nine times. He seemed to appreciate how hard his mother worked and avoided asking her for money for clothing or other necessities. When he needed some money, he "just mugged someone."

These and an endless number of other cases illustrate that the system based on a philosophy of rehabilitation does not work, especially with violent offenders. Almost all states were allowed to transfer juveniles to adult court under special conditions. New laws are aimed at helping control violent crime in a variety of ways. Many states now make the transfer from juvenile court to adult court automatic in cases where certain crimes are committed. The old laws usually gave the judge or the prosecutor the discretion to transfer if the particular youth had exhausted the benefits of the juvenile justice system. Some new laws provide for fixed sentences for certain youths even though they are tried as juveniles.

When juveniles are transferred to adult court, they lose some of the advantages they had in the juvenile system. For example, adult trials are not confidential. And, a permanent record of the proceedings may follow the defendent throughout adult life. The young person is labeled a criminal rather than a delinquent.

New laws have helped to appease many of those who feared the violent young. These people were satisfied as long as the violent offenders were quickly removed from the streets. They were unconcerned that children as young as thirteen were considered beyond hope.

But with these new laws came problems. The Juvenile Offender Law was passed in New York State in August of 1978, and it was put into effect almost at once. With this law, a thirteen-year-old who was convicted of second-degree murder faced a mandatory sentence of at least five years to life. Such a child could be placed in a prison system without rehabilitative services. A child wrongly accused might wait a long time before being tried in adult court, where things move slowly. Imagine how destructive a period of detention in the criminal justice system would be to an innocent child.

There were other concerns after the passage of the Juvenile Offender Law. Many thoughtful people questioned how these juveniles could be helped by a system that was already unable to care properly for children who were being held in secure detention.

Not all children sent to adult court remained there. The law allowed for a transfer back to the juvenile court if the adult criminal court judge felt that the youth would not benefit from adult court treatment.

People who thought the new law of trying juveniles as

adults would quickly remove the young people from the
streets were mistaken. Many young people were free on
bond while they waited to be tried. In addition, the increased
due process protections afforded adults often resulted in
acquittals. What's more, the first time a youth is tried in
adult court, he or she may be considered a first offender in
spite of a long history of criminal offenses. Many of the
juveniles being tried as adults are given probation. Obviously, the Juvenile Offender Law that was passed in New York
State in 1978 has not solved the problem of violent crime.
Some changes have already been made in it. But there is no
easy answer to the violent offender problem, and much more
emphasis is being placed on searching for solutions than in
the past.

Some legal scholars, law enforcement officers, judges,
and others who are concerned with the problems created by
violent offenders and with the violent offenders themselves
suggest that much would be gained by the decriminalization
of status offenders. They feel that there is convincing
evidence that the "overprocessing" of status offenders is
both harmful to them and to the system as a whole.
Certainly, it reduces the amount of time and money that is
available to deal with violent or serious offenders.

A three-year study of the New York City Family Court
that was released in 1981 monitored 230 status offenders and
about 270 delinquents. The researchers found that about 9
percent of the status offenders were placed under supervision, but only about half as many of the delinquents were
placed in institutions. No wonder it has been suggested that
a child can get more attention from the court by skipping
school than by robbing a bank. About 73 percent of the
delinquents had their cases dismissed, even though 93
percent of the accused were charged with new offenses while
awaiting the disposition of their original offenses.

The Family Courts receives much criticism for the revolving-door syndrome and for wrist slapping, but judges point out that they have no control over the resources that are available for treatment. A judge cannot compel an institution to accept a delinquent for treatment, and the delinquent most in need of help is usually not eligible for any existing facility. At a time of decreased funding for social programs, the placement of violent offenders is a special problem.

Dr. Michael Pawel, a psychiatrist at St. Lukes-Roosevelt Hospital Center in New York City and an authority on child care services, suggests that the solution to the problem of dealing with antisocial youths is not more knowledge but more money. Many people agree that the kind of facility needed to treat seriously disruptive young people must be highly structured and provide strict supervision. It must be small enough to feel like home and offer individualized, flexible care. Here violent offenders would be treated almost as children in normal families are, and they would learn gradually to deal with more freedom.

Dr. Pawel believes that the most seriously delinquent children are among the most seriously neglected. They feel that the world hates them, so they hate the world. If one feels worthless, what is there to lose by antisocial behavior?

At a time when many public and private facilities lack funding, such a model facility may seem especially impractical. However, it might save money in the long run. A residence that provides comprehensive care for seventeen potential delinquents for ten years might prevent more than a thousand street crimes during that time. Compare the cost of comprehensive care with the cost of police action, court proceedings, and the detention of the criminals for a thousand street crimes. And consider the cost to the victims.

Donna Hamparin, Manager of the Dangerous Juvenile Offender Study, at the Academy for Contemporary Problems at Ohio State University, suggests the following guidelines should be followed when seriously delinquent youths must be incarcerated:

1.   Close ties to the community to which the youth will return.

2.   A flexible, youthful staff that includes some ex-offenders as role models.

3.   Strict enforcement of necessary rules; assurance that the facility is law-abiding.

4.   A significant reward structure that allows tangible incentives for realistically attainable goals.

5.   Staff-intensive security programming with minimal use of jail hardware.

6.   Helping roles for residents.

7.   To the fullest extent possible within the constraints, a maximum of choice and decision-making by individuals, with the consequences fully and clearly related to the choices made.

8.   Credible training and remedial education programs.

Donna Hamparin suggests that the damage done to these youths by years of bad experiences cannot be offset by the best of institutional programs. But young people are resilient, and a program such as the one outlined above can allow the restorative processes of nature to work during a respite from the streets. A confinement of this type is not like that of a hospital or warehouse. Rather, it is an attempt to remedy some of the problems of the severely damaged youth, and to allow for his or her successful return to the community.

Henry Singer, Executive Director of the Human Resources Institute of Westport, Connecticut, suggests that the energy of antisocial youths be positively directed in a Youth Conservation Corps Program. Selected young people could be taught building trades and other skills to rebuild inner cities. Abandoned military bases could be used as housing facilities and centers of operation. He believes this would cost taxpayers less money than warehousing youths in "crime factories."

The above ideas are extremely controversial. There are those who consider the punishment model the *only* way to deal with violent offenders. The "get tough" groups and the children's rights groups argue on many points, including whether or not there should be specific sentences for specific crimes and whether or not the records of those who repeat serious offenses while still juveniles should be kept confidential.

The American Bar Association issued a lengthy report on the standards for operation of the juvenile courts and correctional systems. The report recommended that the sentences of juveniles be standardized according to the severity of the offense, the age of the child, and his or her criminal record. It was recommended that the child's social history should not be a factor in determining a disposition.

There are many approaches to dealing with the violent offender, but what works for one delinquent may not work for another. Andrew Vachss and Yitzhak Bakal suggest that present models neither protect the public nor reform the offenders. They propose a five-step program for those who are incarcerated that is designed to socialize them toward more acceptable behavior. Vachss and Bakal reject the medical model of treating offenders, and they reject the notion of rehabilitation since this assumes that there was once a repertoire of behavior that was acceptable. One cannot rehabilitate children to behave acceptably if they never knew how to do so in the first place. The program for training violent youths proposed by Vachss and Bakal is described in their book *The Life-style Violent Juvenile: The Secure Treatment Approach,* which is mentioned in the suggested reading list at the end of this book.

Certainly, the violent offender is one of the difficult problems facing the juvenile justice system today.

6

GANGS AND
JUVENILE JUSTICE

The juvenile justice system deals with large numbers of gang members each day, but the ones who come to its courts are not usually the leaders. What are the structures of today's gangs? How do they differ from the gangs of the fifties and those of earlier days? How can one keep children out of the court system when they are acting under the instructions of gang leaders who are not juveniles? Or can some progress be made by working with the younger members of today's gangs? If the older members can no longer use them and benefit because of the short sentences they receive, will this help to deter them?

The twelve-year-old who appeared before the judge in juvenile court was accused of knifing a teacher. He was part of a small gang whose leaders were above the age of those children seen in juvenile court, but as early as the age of eight, the boy had shown gang orientation. Some teachers called his attitude a rip-off mentality. This boy had terrorized many of his classmates in the past, threatening them so they readily gave up lunch money. Recently, he lost his temper at a teacher who was trying to stop his fight with a member of another gang. This scene, or a similar one, could have happened in a large city today, yesterday, and again the day before.

Few people suggest that one can ever do away with gangs. They offer the security that so many urban children lack and they fill many gaps in the child's life. They supply many of the needs of growing up, such as recognition, the need for new experiences, and the feeling of superiority. Gangs have been called a response to the herd instinct in humans.

Stan Davis, a street-gang worker who founded Chicago's Youth Outreach Program, thinks of the gang as a surrogate parent. He sees it as a friendship where individuals really care about each other and this is a positive aspect. Certainly not all gang activities are bad, but for many gangs, violence is a large part of their world. In some, it is the key to moving up in the gang. The younger members are used to "beat the system," and a term in jail is considered prestigious.

Schools were "neutral turf" in the old days when a major objective of gang activity was defending the turf. But that and other characteristics do not apply to today's gangs, which are terrorizing great numbers of people. What part the juvenile court system can play here is a question that begs an answer. Gang activity existed in the early 1900s; the supergangs of the 1950s were made famous by the mass media for their violence and their ability to protect their own culture in strictly defined boundaries. *West Side Story* was a very popular movie that pictured the gang members in a more romantic light than was realistic. But it did show the importance of turf. After the large influx of blacks and Puerto Ricans to New York and other large northern cities, Irish, Italian, and Jewish groups became fearful that the newcomers would "take over." Their children identified with these fears and established boundaries with certain blocks belonging to their groups. Puerto Ricans who retained their own culture either through fear or choice encouraged the rift. An Italian who walked through a Puerto Rican territory would be beaten, as would a Puerto Rican who walked in Italian territory. Gangs were sworn to revenge any hurt done to a member of their own group and definite rules and regulations were established. Some gang names revealed the ethnic makeup of the group, while others revealed the need of the boys for self-esteem. Uniforms differed only in the patches that were sewn on the black or colorful leather jackets.

In the 1960s, the gangs seemed to disappear. The number of reports of gang activities dwindled and few people heard about them. Some writers even reported that gang activity had disappeared due to job opportunities, interest in politics, and drugs, which sapped the strength of the active, young males. According to a 1981 report by Walter B. Miller, an authority on gangs, violence and other forms of illegal activity by youth gangs in the United States is more widespread than previously supposed. The gangs never reached extinction, but they have changed through the years. For example, school is no longer neutral turf. While there is less formalized structure in the gangs, there is increased use of guns. Less time is spent on gang fighting gang and more on preying against innocents.

Researcher Miller finds that the gang problem is a national crime problem of the first magnitude. Today's juvenile justice system in which the judge acts to protect the best interests of the child leaves much to be desired when that child is a gang member who has committed a violent crime on orders from the leader of his gang.

If you live in a large city, you may be well aware of the

destructive behavior of gangs. Your young brother may confide that he is afraid to use the toilets at school because a gang threatens those who interrupt their dice game, which runs continuously through the school day. You may be afraid to walk in certain parts of the city because of gang activity. Or you may be told where to sit in a lunchroom by members of a gang who will beat you if you refuse to obey their commands.

In some schools, activities such as assemblies, after-school athletics, and Friday night dances have been canceled because of the fear of gang violence. Teachers are known to lock classroom doors to keep roaming gangs from stopping by to signal a friend to leave the class. In Philadelphia, where gang activity is known to be especially large, a member of the Board of Education reports that the impact of gang activity is felt in many ways, especially in secondary schools. One of these is a climate of fear and anxiety that is reducing attendance and learning throughout the schools. The mental health of those students who want to remain in school without joining gangs is affected. The following incidents occurred in one year in the Philadelphia public schools: 278 students and 176 teachers were assaulted, and over 100 students and teachers were reported robbed. Nationwide, there are annual reports of 100 murders, 70,000 assaults on teachers, and hundreds of thousands of assaults on students. These reports, educators say, are only the tip of the iceberg.

The destruction of school property as the result of gang violence has been estimated at a cost of hundreds of millions of dollars each year. In some schools, more money was spent as a result of vandalism than was spent on textbooks. Just the cost of replacing the windows in schools in one large city has been equated with the amount necessary to build a new school. Teachers report that students bring a wide variety of weapons to school. Guns, knives, karate sticks, razor blades, kung fu sticks, and other kinds of weapons are found in lockers and, in many cases, are in use.

Many school authorities insist that the number of violent incidents in schools is grossly underestimated. Perhaps as many as two thirds of school crimes go unreported for a variety of reasons. The lack of reporting has been called the "Velvet Cover-up." Teachers and principals do not like to admit that they cannot handle the discipline problems in their schools partly for fear of losing jobs, and partly for fear of becoming victims themselves. Some teachers who report crimes claim that they are harassed by principals. Others say the system of handling complaints about juveniles is inefficient.

One security chief, Richard Green of Los Angeles, complains that the children who create problems are rewarded with more attention than the average student who just tries to get an education. But he feels that all the programs in the world cannot help a seventeen-year-old who has been arrested sixty-five times. Society failed such a child way back when he got into trouble the first time.

The actual causes of delinquency and vandalism in and out of schools are the subject of much debate, but one cause in large cities on the East and West coasts is the presence of youthful organized gangs that operate within a school system. A security director for a city school system sent the following report to the Subcommittee to Investigate Juvenile Delinquency, which reported it to the Committee on the Judiciary of the United States Senate in 1975:

Although the number of gang members in proportion to the overall student population in most schools is minimal, the trouble they cause

is at times cataclysmic. Students are robbed,
intimidated, raped, bludgeoned and sometimes
fatally wounded. Teachers and other adults in
the schools are threatened and on occasions,
physically assaulted. The peace of any school
is breached and the learning climate seriously
polluted by gang activity, however slight.

In some schools, gang activity is so intense
that it is necessary for school security officers
and the local police to escort one gang through
the territory of a rival gang at dismissal time.
At certain schools, Safety Corridors have been
established which provide safe passage for
neutral students under the protection of school
security personnel and police through the hostile
territory. Needless to say, these measures
provide, at best, temporary relief. They do not
begin to attack the root causes of the problem.

There is no simple answer to the root causes of the problem.
Before searching for the causes, the extent of the problem
had to be recognized and it was not until recent years that
such was the case. Walter B. Miller collected data on the
number of gangs and law-violating groups in the United
States and found that the number of members was equivalent to about one-fifth of the number of adolescent males in
2,100 cities and towns with populations of 10,000 and over.
This does not mean that the gang members are evenly
distributed; some cities have more gangs and law-violating
groups than others. But gang members, whose activities are
usually more destructive than those of law-violating group
members, comprise only about seven percent.

In an earlier study, Miller set out to test the validity of

certain assumptions that have a bearing on gangs and juvenile justice and injustice. For example, it has been claimed that the age span of gang members is spreading so that children as young as six and seven are engaging in violent gang activity, while men in their twenties and thirties are playing a much larger role in gangs. Miller found that while there has been some expansion in the age range in both directions, preliminary research indicates that the predominant age range lies somewhere between twelve and twenty-one.

Another claim is that gangs are moving out of the inner city slums and into middle-class suburbs. Miller reports, however, that the primary focus of gang activity remains in the slum sections of a city. Slums and ghettos of some metropolitan areas have moved from the center to the "outer city" where they form a ring around cities, or to formerly middle-class neighborhoods in the suburbs.

The claim that females are more deeply involved in gangs appears false, too. But it is true that ethnic groups still hang together and this element seems to play an important part. Black and Hispanic gangs have replaced many of those made up of children of Irish and Italian blue-collar workers, but a few exceptions exist in which the same gangs go back through several generations. In these, a boy may belong to the same gang his father and grandfather once belonged to. One of the surprising finds in Miller's report was the increase in the number of youths from Asian backgrounds who were involved in gang activity.

Police reports on gang fights in New York's Chinatown help to substantiate this report. A recent flare-up between two rival gangs has been reported. When such an incident occurs, there is the same type of cover-up that one finds in cases of school violence, but the degree of cover-up is even greater. No one will admit knowing anything about a shooting or fight. Even a victim with a bullet still in his hand may refuse to answer a single question. One night after twenty shots were fired in an area, residents said they did not know a shooting had occurred. While they say they have no problems with youth gangs, people appear to be very uncomfortable when questioned by the police. Extortion by the gangs from merchants for "protection" appears to be one reason for silence, which makes the problem of violent gangs especially difficult.

Although the ethnic quality of gangs still exists, today's gangs appear to be more concerned with the question of who is going to control revenue rather than the "pride of walking down my block." Since gangs appear to be more violent today than ever before, the number of victims increases and the entire juvenile justice system has a larger number of lawbreakers to cope with.

Since the illegal activity of members of youth gangs and groups represents a crime problem of major importance, with little hope that it will decrease, research into causes and ways to cope is desperately needed along with action to help put that information into operation. According to James Haskins, author of *Street Gangs: Yesterday and Today,* "No one wants to be 'nobody,' no one wants to be poor, no one wants to live forever amid the hopelessness of the ghetto. As long as these conditions exist, the street gang will continue to exist."*

According to some authorities, the boys who join street gangs have not adapted to society. According to others, these young people are in the wrong place at the wrong time

---

*From *Street Gangs: Yesterday and Today* © 1974 by James Haskins. Reprinted by permission of Hastings House.

and studies such as Miller's do little to actually help the gang situation. They feel money could be better spent on programs that bring positive results than on talk of locking up the lawbreakers. People who are paid to produce research are not always aware of the many positive results that have been achieved by and for former gang members. Not all juvenile gangs act like tribes at war against each other and the world. For many young people, association with a group means positive action rather than profound alienation from society.

Rage and violence have been called tortured ways of reaching out for help. This is the only way some young people know as a way of bringing about change. Gang workers call for better youth services to help them bring about a decrease in the epidemic of violence caused by gangs in cities and by revolting youth in rural and suburban areas. When the rate of delinquency is so very large and when the juvenile justice system appears to be so vastly inadequate, the problem is one for everybody. Locking up the violent offenders may protect society from those who are causing the trouble for a short period of time, providing all can be locked up, but judges and others point out that long ago pickpockets continued to work among the people who were watching a pickpocket being hanged. Punishment, even the most severe, was no deterrent.

Certainly, no one knows the answers to the complicated problem of street gangs. Blame has been placed on individuals, on economic and social environment, on schools that do not provide meaningful values and hopes for the future. The schools, in turn, blame the gangs for creating an environment in which learning is impossible. One thing on which people do agree is the need for more staffing in the juvenile justice system, for more understanding of the problems and funding to do something about them.

7

GIRLS IN TROUBLE

The girls who act as gang members, or who support gang members in their activities, often find their way into the juvenile system. However, arrests of female gang members have been fewer than those of males, and separate female gangs are rare. While the males engage in the main violent activities, such as looting, arson, and other property crimes along with beatings, muggings, rapings, and shootings, the girls are usually less active in auxiliaries or branches of the main gang. Even those girls who are full members of gangs that include both sexes are usually the weapons carriers or participants in less violent activities than the boys. As with the boys, getting out of a gang is difficult. Boys are severely beaten for leaving the gang. Girls who want to get out must submit to sexual activity with the entire gang, even though girl members, auxiliary or otherwise, are usually relatives of or romantically involved with one of the boys in the gang.

While boys make up about 90 percent of gang population, many girls, in and out of gangs, find themselves in trouble with the law. If girls are not playing an increasingly important part in gang violence, what is responsible for the apparent increase in violent acts by females? What part does the new feminism play in this? In some recent years, the number of cases of girls' delinquency handled by courts in the United States has shown an increase while the number of cases for boys has decreased. The boy-girl ratio, which was much greater for boys in the past, has begun to narrow. However, it has become apparent that the nature of the offenses committed by girls is generally less violent.

In the past, a great majority of the girls who have been brought to court have been charged with status offenses, conduct that would not be criminal if committed by adults. As new laws are put into action, the status offenders may not be institutionalized, and girls will not be brought to court for such things as truancy. But much time may pass before this situation changes throughout the nation.

Most of today's programs for female delinquents are still rooted in archaic Victorian traditions. Often morals are considered more important than the rights or welfare of girls. While female roles are changing, ways to redirect the energies of delinquent girls have not kept pace. The time is long overdue for focusing adequate resources on the problems unique to girls in trouble.

Consider the case of Beth. This sixteen-year-old runaway was rejected by her foster mother after she announced that she was pregnant and had no intention of marrying or of giving up her baby. Her foster mother alternated between nagging and tears. Before this, she had been more understanding than any of a long series who had mothered Beth in the past, but she resented the pregnancy and disagreed with Beth, who felt strongly about keeping her baby. Beth did not want this baby to move from home to home the way she had done. She wanted this baby to know a real mother, to have one family, and that would be Beth.

But keeping a baby when one is sixteen years old is not without problems. What is best for the baby? What is best for Beth? Beth felt that she could manage if she had a place where she could keep her baby, go to school to learn to type, then get a job and place the baby in a day-care center. For a time, Beth found refuge in a shelter that was willing to care for her and her baby while she earned her high school diploma. But after that, Beth must find another way to keep herself and her child.

Not all girls who keep their babies find the kind of psychological and financial support they need. Some girls find a sense of security in the closeness of their tiny babies, much the way they felt when they held their dolls and teddy bears. They do not think of the years ahead when the baby will grow up and demand the kind of care they may not be able to give. While an unwed mother is not considered delinquent, she often finds herself at the mercy of the court. Sometimes a financial problem leads to shoplifting or prostitution.

Sometimes one of a girl's parents claims she is incorrigible either because she is pregnant or may become so, and makes her a ward of the state. If she is lucky, she may be placed in a foster home, but such placement is more difficult for girls in their teens than for younger girls and boys.

Suppose you follow a social worker in a large city who is trying to help girls before they reach juvenile court. You find many rootless children living in abandoned buildings amid the rubble. Thelma is a ragged and dirty eleven-year-old slumped in the doorway of one of the buildings. She jumps with fright as you and the social worker approach her. She has good reason not to trust adults, for her stepfather abused her sexually and her mother would not listen to her, believing only the stepfather. Sexual assault is the leading type of abuse among female children. Thelma is just one of

about two million children in the United States who are
being sexually abused by parents, guardians, or commercial
ventures. Thelma ran away from home three weeks ago, and
she has managed to survive on odds and ends of food given
to her by local merchants who know her. At this time, she
refuses to talk with the social worker who offers help.

Upstairs in the same building you find the unheated and
barren apartment that fourteen-year-old Shirley calls home.
Shirley is an abused child who finds safety in the darkness of
the abandoned building. She listens to the music from radios
in apartments across the way and watches the traffic from a
slit in the boarded windows of the apartment, which she has
decorated with scraps of materials and graffiti. Shirley's
body still shows signs of the beating that her mother gave her
when she came home late one night. Her mother insisted she
had been staying with a boy, but Shirley could not explain
her actions or her feelings to her mother, who was so full of
rage. She had already been beaten so many times that
nothing seemed to matter anymore. It did not help much to
know that the same kind of treatment had caused the scar on
her mother's face when *she* was growing up. Beating was the
only way her mother knew of coping with unwanted
behavior. And sometimes, the beatings came for reasons
that Shirley could not understand.

Shirley is so pathetic you wonder how anyone could
mistreat her. The social worker with you says that huge
numbers of children in the United States are abused or
neglected, according to the National Center for Child Abuse
and Neglect. Many children are discovered abused through
frequent hospitalization for injuries that do not fit explana-
tions. Suspicious doctors and nurses report these situations
to social agencies. Shirley's mother, if she can be reached,
might be helped by a group called Parents Anonymous,
where she will be offered a treatment program she can accept

and respond to. This is one of a number of self-help groups that help parents express angry feelings at times of crisis without the risk of exposure or public interference. Groups of parents join together to form hotlines and group meetings where they share their feelings with others who are experiencing the same problems. Through participation in such groups, parents improve their self-images and their relationships, which, in turn, helps in their relationships with their children. They learn not to feel helpless and fearful. They find outlets for their anger and rage that do not harm their children. But before a social worker can help Shirley's family, she must persuade her mother that joining such a group can be important for her to retain custody of Shirley and that it will not result in social exile. If the social worker succeeds, she may be helping in many ways, for children whose mothers and fathers abuse them will often become parents who abuse the next generation. In the meantime, Shirley will fend for herself, begging for food from neighbors and eventually joining the many girls who survive by entertaining men for a fee, the very thing her mother feared. Sooner or later she will be involved with the juvenile justice system.

Nine-year-old Julie ran away from a home where her alcoholic father and heroin-addict mother gave her little love or attention. She sleeps in a gang's clubhouse where the boys feed her and treat her well. She would stay with them, enjoying their parties and their friendship, if she was not so sick. But the social worker offers her medical care and a home with other children who are her own age, so she agrees to leave the security of the gang. They had never counted her as one of them, anyhow, and she felt uncomfortable about taking their food. As you leave her at the shelter, you wonder whether or not Julie will adapt to the ways there. She has lived most of her life without any rules and she angers easily. While care and love are offered to her, the number of people being housed gives little time for individual problems. And Julie has never learned to trust adults or accept their love.

For many of the rootless girls in the cities, life is a hopelessly difficult cycle of the street, juvenile hall, shelters, foster homes, and the streets again. This is not true for all, for the interaction of forces working for them and their own efforts may bring a new kind of life. Those who have run away from the deep sorrow in their homes in search of love are sometimes lucky enough to learn how to relate to a different environment. But many who have known only hate or who have their own emotional problems find more problems ahead.

Some of the girls who live on the streets enjoy the money that they earn in "parlors" or by being "on call" for a while, but some of the thousands of girls who live this way in any big city give up in search of a better life because they find themselves caught in an endless cycle that brings them nowhere. An estimated two thousand girls are on the streets of New York City alone, and another two thousand girls are "on call" or regularly employed in houses of prostitution. While those girls who are under eighteen often come in contact with the juvenile justice system, comparatively few are actually helped by it unless they are ready to help themselves. Even then, unbelievably difficult situations may interfere with their futures.

Girls who run away in the city seldom go far from home or use the hotlines that are available. Runaways from suburbs and rural areas sometimes migrate to the cities. On their way, or when they reach their destinations, many of these girls call one of the national hotline numbers: National Runaway Switchboard—800-621-4000 toll-free from anywhere in the United States except Illinois, or 800-972-6004 toll-free from anywhere in Illinois. Or, Operation: Peace of Mind—800-231-6946 toll-free from anywhere in the United States except Texas, 800-392-3352 toll-free from anywhere in Texas except Houston, or 524-3821 local from anywhere in Houston.

These runaway hotline numbers are helpful to both boys and girls but they are especially important to girls. The law for runaways and incorrigibles has always been the same for boys and girls, but in the past more than twice as many girls have been charged with breaking them. How new laws will change this situation remains to be seen.

The hotlines themselves do not necessarily discriminate between boys and girls. They provide anonymous help for those who call in several ways: They send messages home to parents without telling where the runaway is, and they will relay a message from home to the runaway. They also help by directing a boy or girl to the nearest runaway house where free shelter and other help is provided for a limited period of time.

For many runaway girls, family counseling or other help can make life more bearable at home when parents want them. In many cases two generations just do not know how to communicate with one another and the interaction grows unpleasantly out of proportion to the problems. The following is such a case. It happened in a juvenile court in northern California when a girl tried to defend her mother against her grandparents who were upset because of the mother's sexual involvement.

Naomi, age thirteen, was charged with assault on her grandmother, and the case against her was aggressively presented by the probation officer. Under his questioning, the grandmother angrily stated that the girl had pushed her and struck her without provocation in the early morning hours in her own house. This had badly upset the grandfather who came downstairs on the scene shortly thereafter. He verified his wife's version of the events.

But slowly under cross-examination by the defense attorney, it became clear that the girl had done no more than push her grandmother down into a chair to compel her to listen to her. This was a reaction to events of the previous evening when in the girl's presence the grandmother had called her mother a whore, mainly because she was associating with an Indian. The two had gone to San Francisco the night in question. The girl was badly disturbed, brooded about the remark, finally phoned her grandmother to demand a face-to-face explanation in her house, where the alleged "assault" occurred. Further questioning made it fairly clear that the court action was one of a long series of harassments to remove the mother and girl from a small house owned by the grandmother.

The following is another example of what happened to a girl, this time because of parents' concern for her as a girl. Had she been a boy, their actions might have been quite different.

One April day, Susan L. was brought to juvenile hall by her parents in the hope that a probation officer could prevent any further misbehavior and dissuade Susan from wanting to leave home and live in a foster home. At this time Susan was a very attractive fifteen-year-old.

According to the probation officer who handled the situation and wrote the intake report:

> *During Easter vacation her father hit her for wearing a girlfriend's skirt, calling her a liar and a bitch. The parents indicated they did not want Susan wearing the girl's skirt, that they do not like Susan in those kind of clothes. Susan admits that she deliberately turned up the hem of her*

*already short dress in order to be kicked out of
the house by her parents so she could come to
juvenile hall. She stated that they are constantly
fighting and picking on her over everything.*

The probation officer offered to place Susan on informal
probation, without going to court. She refused, stating that
going home would not do any good and that she would
rather stay in juvenile hall. After a short stay in juvenile hall,
however, Susan changed her mind and returned home on
informal probation.

A second probation officer was assigned to supervise
Susan. On April 25—one week after the initial trip to
juvenile hall—this officer reported the results of her initial
home visit:

*This officer stated to Susan the terms and
conditions of probation and made specific
emphasis on the fact that she was required to
obey her parents' wishes and she was not to leave
the home without their permission. This officer
also advised Susan that she would prefer that she
not associate with other children who were on
probation since they seemed to be a very poor
influence on her.*

Two months later, on June 18, the second probation officer
paid another visit to Susan's house because some trouble
had arisen. In her report of this visit, she stated:

*This officer gave Susan quite a lecture about
leaving home without permission and also
remaining away from home overnight. At this
time Susan was placed on restriction for two*

weeks, at the probation officer's recommendation. Her parents felt that this was suitable punishment for what Susan had done. The parents advised the officer that if this happened again, they would most likely not be happy to have her in their home on a permanent basis. The officer advised that if Susan left home without permission again and remained away all night, they should most likely bring her down to juvenile hall for being beyond their control. The parents felt that Susan was psychologically unstable and felt that there were certain things in her actions and behavior that they felt were abnormal for a girl Susan's age. The officer recommended that if they felt she needed some kind of counseling or help that they take advantage of psychiatric services.

On October 27, Susan was released from informal probation. She had been seen six times over a six-month period. The second probation officer in the release summary stated:

At this time the situation seems to have stabilized somewhat: However, it could blow up at any time. This officer would say that Susan's adjustment has been marginal and the prognosis only fair.

Three months later (the next January) Susan was again brought to juvenile hall by her parents for being beyond their control.

A third probation officer handled the situation and wrote the intake report:

*Mother seems to be extremely cold and is not
realistic in attempting to understand this minor.
Father appears to have the same difficulty but
appears to care for the minor more than the
mother. Both parents are complimentary about
the girl's intelligence and future but seem
inadequate in helping her.*

After several days in the juvenile hall, Susan was again
placed on informal probation and the case assigned to a
fourth probation officer.

Five weeks later (early in March) Susan ran away
again. A fifth probation officer screened the case and
referred it back to the fourth probation officer.

Probation officer number four tried to work the
situation out, but since the parents refused to have Susan
back home, had to refer the matter to court.

At the detention hearing two days later, the judge
ordered that Susan be detained and that a psychological
examination be performed.

The clinical psychologist assigned to this evaluation
had this to say in his report to the court:

*The psychological interview and the data
available within the file indicate long-term
difficulties within this family which will have to
be solved in some way other than through strict
authoritarianism on the part of the father. Even
the mother has apparently recognized that the
father is unfairly rigid at times and upon occasion
has lied for this girl. The mother has given Susan
permission to do some things while keeping them
from the father simply because the mother feels*

*that the girl is entitled to it. This of course can
be quite misleading, offering many forms of
inconsistency.... This examiner is of the belief
that without family counseling this girl stands
little chance of making an adequate adjustment
within her own home.... Replacing this girl in
her own home as a Ward of the Court without
any form of professional intervention or assistance will do no more than to encourage the
parents to further inhibit this girl's behavior and
at the same time make it almost impossible for
her to operate in any way other than a rebellious
manner. To prevent such a failure, this examiner
feels that outside professional help will be the
only method which can assist the family in
correcting the distortions that exist between
them. Probationary services, per se, will be of
little value in this instance, as the parents, particularly the father, will merely rely upon the
probation officer (the judge) to enforce whatever
rules her father deems necessary. This is a family
problem with the girl showing the symptoms. In
order to help this girl and her symptoms, the
difficulties within the family must be worked
out.*

The probation officer writing the court report—who coin-
cidentally was officer number two, the first to supervise
Susan—stated:

*Susan will continue to have difficulty in the
home unless the probation officer is extremely
supportive of the parents' position and makes*

the minor realize and accept the fact that as long
as she is residing in their home that she will have
to abide by their rules.

After considering these reports the court adjudged Susan a ward of the court and returned her home on March 26. The court recommended a change in probation officers and also recommended that the minor and parents seek professional counseling.

On April 10, probation officer number six was assigned to the case. On April 15, Susan was booked back into juvenile hall for truancy.

Probation officer number seven handled the intake and referred the matter to court. In his intake report he stated:

The minor has been advised that if she is again
truant from school, that she will be picked up by
the court officer and booked into juvenile hall.

On April 29, Susan was again booked into juvenile hall for truancy. Probation officer number eight handled the intake and referred the matter to probation officer number two who had written the first court report and was writing the court report on the previous truancy. At the detention hearing held the same day, Susan was ordered detained. One month later, on March 23, the court continued her as a ward and returned her home with a requirement that she work six days on the county juvenile work project.

On July 4, two months later, Susan again ran away from home, was picked up by the police and taken to juvenile hall. Probation officer number five handled the intake and filed another petition alleging a violation of probation in that the minor ran away from home.

In fifteen months Susan had been booked into juvenile hall six times—all for status offenses—and had spent over thirty days in detention. She had seen eight different probation officers and a clinical psychologist. She had been referred to court on three occasions and appeared before a judge and two referees. Several probation officers, the clinical psychologist, and the court had *recommended on various occasions that the family get professional counseling, but this never happened.* *

The above case took place in Sacramento County in California before the introduction there of an experimental program to divert such cases from juvenile court. The diversion project not only attempts to keep children such as Susan out of juvenile hall, but it also attempts to keep family problems out of the court and offers counseling and help for the family. Such programs are increasing and will be described more fully in a later chapter.

In most areas, there is a double standard of dealing with boys and girls. Parents will often tolerate misbehavior in a son, but they will file a petition for similar behavior of a daughter. As a result of this, large numbers of females have been referred to juvenile courts where they are sentenced to various programs of detention. Harsher penalties have traditionally been handed down to girls than to boys for nonviolent crimes. One theory for this is that the girls must be protected from themselves, based primarily on the fact that girls may become involved in sexual activity.

Has the new feminism with its greater independence and aggressiveness in the daily activities of women played a

---

*Roger Baron and Floyd Feeney, *Juvenile Diversion Through Family Counseling,* Law Enforcement Assistance Administration, 1976, pp.51-52.

part in the alleged increase in female criminality? Some authorities attribute an increase to both the changes in women's personalities and the changes of attitudes toward women. According to another theory, women's crimes may not be increasing as fast as statistics indicate, but police and judicial *dispositions* may make it appear that far more women are involved in crime than in earlier years. In addition to the different handling of female cases, modern and more efficient methods of recording all crimes may be part of the difference. No matter what the reason, the fact remains that the law treats girls and young women differently from boys and young men.

Many authorities who work with girls in trouble are concerned because the traditional methods of dealing with juvenile delinquents appear to be failing more with girls than with boys. According to Mary Kaaren Jolly, Editorial Director of the United States Senate Subcommittee to Investigate Juvenile Delinquency, female delinquents are institutionalized for less serious crimes more often than males, and latest data indicate that they spend, on the average, two months longer in institutions than boys do. After incarceration, they remain on parole for longer periods.

On July 26, 1976, Senator Birch Bayh called attention to some of the recommendations of the International Women's Year Commission, which called for elimination of discrimination based on sex within all levels of the juvenile justice system. They urged federal action on a number of fronts, including many programs to help females who are caught in the juvenile system. This seems especially important in view of the following midwestern study. Of more than eight hundred juvenile court referrals, these proportions were typical: 28 percent of the boys had been brought to court for "unruly offenses," compared with 52 percent of the girls. At the juvenile detention home, running away and sex offenses accounted for 60.7 percent of all the female delinquent referrals; moreover girls on the average stayed there three times as long as boys. Such discrimination based on the sex of status offenders traditionally has been upheld on the grounds of "reasonableness."

In research supplied to the Subcommittee to Investigate Juvenile Delinquency, of the U.S. Senate Judiciary Committee, Senator Bayh points out the following remark that expresses a typical attitude. In responding to facts that confirm gross discrimination against girls, the director of a state institution for girls explained: "Girls, unlike boys, offend more against themselves than against other persons or property." Senator Bayh suggests that what she really meant was that more often girls—as compared to boys—are locked up for engaging in disapproved sexual conduct at an early age; that our society applies the term "promiscuous" to girls but not to boys.

New directions in female correctional programming call for effective rehabilitation and treatment programs designed specifically for the female offender. They call for the assurance that more resources will be available to prevent female delinquency. While the place to start with an individual is before she becomes a delinquent, some girls have gravitated beyond the realm of status offenses. Here is another serious problem.

With the increasing numbers of women as police officers, youth workers, lawyers, and judges, it is hoped that girls in trouble will be treated less paternalistically. It is hoped that decisions about a young girl's actions may be based on the facts that are present rather than the prevailing double standard.

8

EXPLORING DIVERSION

The earlier a child comes into the juvenile justice system the greater the likelihood that the child will develop and continue a delinquent and criminal career. This statement has been made again and again by many authorities. Diversion from juvenile detention and incarceration for those who commit only minor offenses is a basic aim of those who want to improve justice for boys and girls.

Research indicates that over 50 percent of the hundreds of thousands of juveniles who are placed in jails or police lockups each year could be released without serious threat to the community or the court process.

Detention centers are intended to operate as way stations during the interim between the time a child is accused and the time of a hearing if secure custody is needed. Unfortunately detention is often lengthy and the experience is often a very traumatic and demoralizing one for the child.

More punishment, not less, is the cry from many who live in areas where there is a high crime rate among juveniles.

While our communities are entitled to be free of persons who threaten safety, it is self-defeating to ignore the commonsense approach of the old adage that an ounce of prevention is worth a pound of cure.

As they implement the Juvenile Justice and Delinquency Prevention Act of 1974, planners are trying to provide a constructive and workable approach in a joint federal, state, and local effort to control and reverse the alarming rise in juvenile crime. According to Senator Birch Bayh, the act is designed specifically to prevent young people from entering our failing juvenile system and to assist communities in developing humane, sensible, and economic programs for young people already in the system. It provides federal assistance for local, public, and private groups to establish temporary shelter care facilities and counseling services for youths and their families outside the law-enforcement structure.

The programs that are being tried experimentally with the aim of diversion are numerous and varied. The process of diversion can be either a way of preventing juvenile delinquency or a way of reducing penetration into the system. An increasing number of juvenile justice planners and policy makers are investing their hopes of reducing delinquency in diversion programs. There have been a large number of programs that aim to reduce the stigma thought to be attached to those who have been involved in the juvenile justice system in any way. Some authorities even question whether or not there will be a negative labeling of those who have been part of a diversion program.

By one definition, diversion occurs after a youth's initial official contact with an agent of the law and prior to formal sentencing. Some of the programs that call themselves diversion programs are really alternatives to detention or incarceration. But no matter how one defines them, the programs appear to be making a small but good beginning.

At the present time some programs are successful; some are not. Many use rates of repeat offenses to evaluate their programs, and this is questioned by some workers in the field. Here are a few examples of the programs that are being explored.

A number of programs have been so outstanding that they have been helpful for many communities that are searching for better ways to help juveniles and those who come in contact with them. One of these programs is titled Family Crisis Counseling: An Alternative to Juvenile Court. This is a diversion project of Sacramento County Probation Department and the Center on Administration of Criminal Justice of the University of California, Davis, California. It is based on mobilizing the whole family to deal with the problem and on diverting the problem from the courts. Specially trained probation officers meet with the family as soon as possible to provide crisis counseling. The couselor helps to return the boy or girl to a home where, as a result of the counselor's intervention, there is to be a commitment by all family members to work out the problem.

Beginning as an experiment in the fall of 1970, the above program was so successful that the project techniques became standard for all runaway, "beyond control," and incorrigible-type cases in the county. In addition to this, new experiments on testing the possibility of using the same techniques for handling criminal violations such as malicious mischief, petty theft, possession of drugs, and joyriding were introduced.

Suppose Ken is a fifteen-year-old who lives in Sacramento County where he refuses to go to school. He has been absent for four days without excuse and informs his parents that he does not plan to go ever again. According to the law and according to the family's plans for his future, Ken is in trouble. His family says he has fallen into bad company, and they connot control him. So they call the police about the problem and ask the police to help them bring Ken to a juvenile court where he will be committed to a juvenile hall and "kept under control." Rather than this, a trained probation officer comes to the house and discusses the crisis with Ken and his family within one hour of the time the trouble has been reported. He finds that Ken refuses to stay in the same house with his parents, so with both Ken's and the parents' permission, the probation officer finds a place where Ken can stay until his feelings cool.

The next day, Ken and his family sit down with the probation officer and discuss the problems. They try role playing, which is acting out some of their problems with each person in the role of another family member. This helps each individual to see the whole family's problems more objectively. The parents observe that they are paying much more attention to the young baby in the family than they are to Ken. He finds that in the role of a parent, he, too, pays more attention to the new baby than to the person who is playing his role. Some of the hurt feelings come out in the open and even though many problems remain to be solved, the current crisis is over and the parents no longer want to send Ken to juvenile court. In this way, they avoid the strong possibility of Ken's detention overnight in juvenile hall and a probation period lasting from six months to a year.

Ken's family was encouraged to return for a second discussion of problems with the probation officer acting as a counselor. If they wished to do so and the case warranted further sessions, they might have as many as five. But all sessions after the first in this type of program are voluntary.

Projects such as the Sacramento County Diversion Project have four main goals:

1. to reduce the number of cases going to court

2. to reduce the number of repeat offenses

3. to decrease overnight detentions

4. to accomplish these goals at a cost no greater
   than that required for regular processing of
   cases

Success in meeting these goals has been substantial. All cases handled during the first year of the project were followed for a period of twelve months from the initial contact. Those handled by the family crisis counseling approach were compared with cases handled in the usual manner. While both groups had a high rate of repeat conflict with the law, those helped by the diversion project were less apt to repeat violations. The second year of the project appears to have been even more successful than the first. In addition to trying to prevent repeat offenses, the diversion project appears to indicate that the number of court petitions, the number of informal probations, the number of days spent in detention, and the cost of handling the cases were all less than for those not involved in the program. Those who sponsor the project point out that success in avoiding detention helps in two ways. It avoids detention, which is a harmful factor that serves as a school of crime. It also does away with the embittering factor that often makes family reconciliations more difficult than when there is no detention.

Many diversion projects of the above type have been put into action. The Sacramento County Diversion Project is one of the relatively few that have been recognized as exemplary. This means it has passed rigorous screenings that show that there has been overall effectiveness in the reduction of crime or improvement in the operations of the justice system. It also is the kind of program that can be adapted to other places, is efficient when cost is considered, and has been measured for at least a year. It is one in which the project staff cooperated willingly to provide information to other communities.

Another outstanding program is the Neighborhood Youth Resources Center in Philadelphia, Pennsylvania. Here a wide range of services are provided for children who live in a high crime area of the inner city. In addition to its role as a community center, this program offers a variety of other help, such as counseling for youth on probation, crisis intervention, referrals to cooperating agencies and careful monitoring and follow-up. Arrest rates have been compared with those for boys who lived in a similar high crime area and have been found to be significantly lower where the Neighborhood Youth Resource Center is functioning.

Another exemplary project of special interest was established in Champaign-Urbana, Illinois. Here, young people who have contact with police that would normally lead to the juvenile court are referred to a project that involves undergraduates at the University of Illinois. Volunteers from the college receive training and supervision from experienced psychologists, an activity that continues throughout their involvement in the program. College credit in psychology is one of the rewards for the volunteers. Working with these young people is another type of reward, for the volunteers find the experience worthwhile.

Children selected for the program have had several police contacts during the year prior to the project. Another group of children who had a similar number of police contacts are used as controls to see whether or not there is diversion power in what the volunteers are doing. Each young person is assigned to one volunteer for a period of four-and-a-half months. Two approaches are used. One is a contract technique in which the boy or girl signs a contract with a parent or a teacher that spells out specific obligations that each party must fulfill. Obligations are based on the assessment of the student volunteer who helps in carrying out the program. Examples of obligations are obeying curfew hours or doing household chores. The second approach involves a technique through which the volunteer introduces the child to resources in the community and encourages their use. Mental health, education, welfare, and health resources are included.

In the first year of the Champaign-Urbana program, results appeared to be very positive. In the experimental group, where the average number of police contacts in the year prior to the project was 2.21, the number of police contacts during the project dropped to 0.46. In the control group, the number of contacts was 2.25 for both years.

Those who plan diversion programs need to make special efforts to guarantee that persons diverted from court would not have gone there if not involved in their programs. In some cases, diversion programs may bring more children into the system. But for many, involvement in such programs appears to provide a better chance of finding meaningful help when it is needed and less chance to travel through the turnstile that leads in and out of the juvenile justice system.

9

SEARCHING FOR ANSWERS

Obviously there are no easy answers to the problems of juvenile justice and injustice. The problems might be compared to a tangle of yarn that was interwoven in a complicated mesh for a period of many years. Attempts to carry out new programs are the untangling of just a few threads. Juvenile injustice is an unpleasant subject, and many people would like to avoid even thinking about it, let alone trying to correct some of the inequities. Awareness of what has been happening and what is happening is often confined to a few sensational stories of mistreatment which are reported from time to time in the mass media. Then the problems are forgotten.

Many people who are aware of injustices presented volumes of testimony during the three years of research prior to the passage of the Juvenile Justice and Delinquency Prevention Act of 1974. This measure had strong bipartisan support as reflected in the 88 to 1 vote in the United States Senate and the 329 to 20 vote in the House of Representatives. But many years after its passage, one finds that progress is slow. Reduced funding has added to the many problems.

There are judges who feel the old way is best. Not all judges have case loads that enable them to spend just a brief time with each child's problems. In some rural areas, it is not uncommon for a judge to make himself available in the middle of the night when a delinquent needs help. So one can see that laws that are excellent for some places cause problems in others. And even where the laws would provide help that is so desperately needed, funding is not adequate. Some situations are being improved by reducing the case load in courts through the handling of status offenders in diversion projects as mentioned in the last chapter and through other approaches. But those who search for answers have far to go.

Even today, it is not uncommon to find a neglected child being held in a correctional facility for many years while a serious offender is back on the streets within a short time. The Chicago Legal Aid Society has been involved with a case of a neglected child that illustrates the above point. John was made a ward of the state at the age of five because his parents were dead and there was no one to care for him. Between his fifth and fifteenth birthdays, John lived in many places. He spent three months in a pretrial detention home in Chicago, then he spent a year in a foster home. This was followed by a month in a pretrial detention center, two months in a foster home, about a year in an orphanage, several months in a foster home, then eight months in an institution for neglected children. At this institution, John showed some delinquent behavior. He was expelled after he allegedly killed a dog. The punishment for this act was having the dog's tail tied around his neck for two weeks and being chained to his bed for several days. Then John was placed in a state mental hospital for two years, even though the staff at the hospital continually insisted that he was not in need of mental health care. After this, John spent a year in a private charitable institution, three months in a pretrial detention center for juveniles, and at the age of fifteen he was committed to the Department of Corrections for allegedly slapping a two-hundred-pound guard at the pretrial detention center.

If one could read a book about all the happenings in John's life, one might wonder that he had not become a violent offender long before the age of fifteen, although there were undoubtedly many kind people in his environment to help balance those who were cruel to him.

Consider conditions at one state school where juvenile justice planners are having to separate status offenders from those who have committed more serious criminal acts. The remark is sometimes made that after a child has been in the school for a while the staff cannot tell which child is the neglected, abused, or status offender and which has been more delinquent. One might ask why this is so. If staff members and other authorities were exposed to delinquent children when they were young, might they acquire some of their types of behavior? Might John, the boy described above, have avoided delinquency if he had grown up in a home situation where he was the recipient of continuous love and care? The words *juvenile injustice* seem quite appropriate for John. He seems to typify the child who spent many years in custody simply because he was a victim of the system.

Ronald, on the other hand, seems to have been able to get out of the system again and again. One finds him, at age nineteen, attacking the elderly. This time his case came to the attention of the public due to an unusual situation in which his juvenile records were brought to light. This was done to influence a judge who was setting bail at five hundred dollars in the case of a robbery when Ronald was considered a nineteen-year-old adult in the fall of 1976. Senator Ralph J. Marino, Chairman of the New York State Senate's Committee on Crime, broke the rules of confidentiality of family court records to introduce the defendant's long background of juvenile delinquency. The information that he supplied illustrates the revolving-door aspect of the juvenile justice system.

Ronald, according to reports, had first entered the system at the age of eight. Between that time and the time he became sixteen, his criminal career brought him to the attention of the juvenile court sixty-seven times. One of these encounters was indeed serious. He was accused, at age sixteen, of robbing and beating a ninety-two-year-old man, who died four or five days later. Ronald's attack on the elderly again brought him to adult court when he was arrested at age nineteen for the robbing and beating of an eighty-two-year-old woman. It was at this point that the judge in adult court was asked to consider his juvenile record before setting bail.

What is the full story of Ronald's life? Many people may have tried to help him adjust to society, and many others may have played a part in his maladjustment. No one knows how much of his problem was his fault or how much was the fault of others. What is known is that he was part of a system based, theoretically at least, on feelings of benevolence in which young people should be treated and not punished. In these days of extensive violent crime by juveniles, cases such as Ronald's made people swing from the attitude of considering only the "best interests of the child" toward considering the needs of the community for protection.

Repeat offenses are not uncommon in the juvenile justice system, although the sixty-seven repeats of Ronald may be an unusually high number. *Recidivism,* or repeated relapse into crime, is even greater among juveniles than among adult offenders. Among juveniles the rate has been estimated at 74 to 85 percent while for adults the rate estimates range from 25 to 70 percent.

In one study, which was done by Professor Marvin Wolfgang, 6 percent of ten thousand boys he studied in Philadelphia were responsible for more than half the recorded delinquent acts and about two thirds of the violent crime committed by the whole group. But it is this serious crime that concerns society most.

Searching for answers that are just in protecting the victims of crime and protecting the young while suppressing their criminality seems an impossible task. But the search must go on at a faster pace and on a wider front. While the controversy between crime prevention and youth protection is not new and not easily solved, an increasing number of people are aware of many injustices in the juvenile justice system.

Justice for the young *is* happening on thousands of fronts every day. The children who are helped by the juvenile justice system through programs that give them educational help, solid work experience through vocational probation, counseling, and other help seldom make the headlines, but they are there. But so are the children who suffer injustice. Who speaks for them? Only a relatively few of them make the headlines.

In recent years, many groups have concerned themselves with the problems of juvenile justice and injustice.

Some are the National Council of Jewish Women, the Young Men's and Women's Christian Associations, the American Association of University Women, the General Federation of Women's Clubs, and the League of Women Voters. They have been called the eyes, ears, and conscience of local communities.

Many communities are experimenting with local programs in their efforts to curb juvenile crime, and, in some cases, their success has been outstanding. Programs such as Umoja, in Philadelphia, have successfully met the needs of some of the toughest gang members. They provide hope instead of despair through job development and through activities geared to uplifting the spirit of the community.

Police units who advise the elderly who are being terrorized by youths tell them not to fight back if attacked. This is good advice. But for the great majority of the population there are ways to fight back through improvement in the quality of the juvenile justice system. A first step is awareness of injustices and the need for change in a system geared primarily to react to youthful offenders rather than prevent youthful offense.

Today, you may find your fifth-grade neighbor doing homework on an article about a nine-year-old murderer who had been in and out of institutions many times. This article appears in his or her grade level newspaper and the problem of juvenile justice and injustice is one for his or her class. From age 11 to 111, this subject is one for concern and involvement.

10

APPENDIXES

I. FINDINGS AND DECLARATION OF PURPOSE JUVENILE JUSTICE DELINQUENCY PREVENTION ACT OF 1974

Findings

The Congress hereby finds that

1. juveniles account for almost half the arrests for serious crimes in the United States today;

2. understaffed, overcrowded juvenile courts, probation services, and correctional facilities are not able to provide individualized justice or effective help;

3. present juvenile courts, foster and protective care programs, and shelter facilities are inadequate to meet the needs of countless abandoned and dependent children, who, because of this failure to provide effective services, may become delinquents;

4. existing programs have not adequately responded to the particular problems of the increasing numbers of young people who are addicted to or who abuse drugs, particularly nonopiate or polydrug abusers;

5. juvenile delinquency can be prevented through programs designed to keep students in elementary and secondary schools through the prevention of unwarranted and arbitrary suspensions and expulsions;

6. states and local communities which experience directly the devastating failures of the juvenile justice system do not presently have sufficient technical expertise or adequate resources to deal comprehensively with the problems of juvenile delinquency; and

7. existing federal programs have not provided the direction, coordination, resources, and leadership required to meet the crisis of delinquency.

Congress finds further that the high incidence of delinquency in the United States today results in enormous annual cost and immeasurable loss of human life, personal security, and wasted human resources and that juvenile delinquency constitutes a growing threat to the national welfare requiring immediate and comprehensive action by the federal government to reduce and prevent delinquency.

Purpose

It is the purpose of this Act

1. to provide for the thorough and prompt evaluation of all federally assisted juvenile delinquency programs;

2. to provide technical assistance to public and private agencies, institutions, and individuals in developing and implementing juvenile delinquency programs;

3. to establish training programs for persons, including professionals, paraprofessionals, and volunteers, who work with delinquents or potential delinquents, or whose work or activities relate to juvenile delinquency programs;

4. to establish a centralized research effort on the problems of juvenile delinquency, including an information clearing-house to disseminate the findings of such research and all data related to juvenile delinquency;

5. to develop and encourage the implementation of national standards for the administration of juvenile justice, including recommendations for administrative, budgetary, and legislative action at the federal, state, and local level to facilitate the adoption of such standards;

6. to assist states and local communities with resources to develop and implement programs to keep students in elementary and secondary schools and to prevent unwarranted and arbitrary suspensions and expulsions; and

7. to establish a federal assistance program to deal with the problems of runaway youth.

It is therefore the further declared policy of Congress to provide the necessary resources, leadership, and coordination 1. to develop and implement effective methods of preventing and reducing juvenile delinquency; 2. to develop and conduct effective programs to prevent delinquency, to divert juveniles from the traditional juvenile justice system and to provide critically needed alternatives to institutionalization; 3. to improve the quality of juvenile justice in the United States; and 4. to increase the capacity of the state and local governments and public and private agencies to conduct effective juvenile justice and delinquency prevention and rehabilitation programs and to provide research, evaluation, and training services in the field of juvenile delinquency prevention.

II. ORGANIZATIONS ENDORSING THE JUVENILE JUSTICE DELINQUENCY PREVENTION ACT OF 1974

American Federation of State, County and Municipal
   Employees
American Institute of Family Relations
American Legion, National Executive Committee
American Parents Committee
American Psychological Association
B'nai B'rith Women
Children's Defense Fund
Child Study Association of America
Chinese Development Council
Christian Prison Ministries
Emergency Task Force on Juvenile Delinquency
John Howard Association
National Alliance on Shaping Safer Cities
National Association of Counties
National Association of Social Workers
National Association of State Juvenile Delinquency
   Program Administrators
National Collaboration for Youth:
     Boys' Clubs of America
     Boy Scouts of America

Camp Fire Girls, Inc.
Federal Executive Service
4-H Clubs
Future Homemakers of America
Girls' Clubs
Girl Scouts of U.S.A.
National Federation of Settlements and Neighborhood
    Red Cross Youth Service Programs
National Jewish Welfare Board
National Board of YWCAs
National Council of YMCAs
National Commission on the Observance of International
    Women's Year Committee on Child Development
National Conference of Criminal Justice Planning
    Administrators
National Conference of State Legislatures
National Council on Crime and Delinquency
National Council of Jewish Women
National Council of Juvenile Court Judges
National Council of Organizations of Children and Youth
National Federation of State Youth Service Bureau
    Associations
National Governors Conference
National Information Center on Volunteers in Courts
National League of Cities
National Legal Aid and Defender Association
National Network of Runaway and Youth Services
National Urban Coalition
National Youth Alternatives Project
Public Affairs Committee, National Association for Mental
    Health, Inc.
Robert F. Kennedy Action Corps
U.S. Conference of Mayors

III.   SOME HELPFUL RESOURCES

American Bar Association
National Legal Resource Center for Child Advocacy and
Protection
1800 M St., N.W., 2nd Floor S.
Washington, D.C. 20036

American Civil Liberties Union Children's Rights Project
132 West 43rd Street
New York, New York 10036

American Friends Service Committee
1501 Cherry Street
Philadelphia, Pennsylvania 19102

Association of Junior Leagues, Inc.
825 Third Avenue
New York, New York 10022

Association on American Indian Affairs, Inc.
432 Park Avenue S.
New York, New York 10016

Children's Defense Fund
1520 New Hampshire Avenue, N.W.
Washington, D.C. 20036

National Commission on Resources for Youth
36 West 44th Street
New York, New York 10036

National Committee for Prevention of Child Abuse

332 South Michigan Avenue, Suite 1250
Chicago, Illinois 60604

National Council of Jewish Women
15 East 26th Street
New York, New York 10010

National Council of Juvenile and Family Court Judges
University of Nevada
P.O. Box 8000
Reno, Nevada 89507

National Council of Negro Women
1819 H Street, N.W., Suite 900
Washington, D.C. 20006

National Council of the Churches of Christ
Child and Family Justice Project
475 Riverside Drive, Room 560
New York, New York 10027

National Council on Crime and Delinquency
Continental Plaza
411 Hackensack Avenue
Hackensack, New Jersey 07801

National Network of Runaway and Youth Services, Inc.
1705 DeSales Street, N.W., 8th floor
Washington, D.C. 20036

National Urban League
500 East 62nd Street
New York, New York 10021

National Youth Work Alliance
1346 Connecticut Avenue, N.W.
Washington, D.C. 20036

National Center for Youth Law
1663 Mission Street, 5th floor
San Francisco, California 94103

IV.   STATE PLANNING AGENCIES

If you are interested in the juvenile justice programs in your
state, you may wish to write to the planning agency that is
the headquarters for your area.

ALABAMA
Alabama Law Enforcement Planning Agency
2863 Fairlane Drive, Suite 49 Executive Park
Montgomery, Alabama 36111

ALASKA
Governor's Commission on the Administration of Justice
Pouch AJ
Juneau, Alaska 99801

ARIZONA
Arizona State Justice Planning Agency
4820 North Black Canyon
Phoenix, Arizona 85017

ARKANSAS
Commission on Crime and Law Enforcement
1515 Building Suite 700
Little Rock, Arkansas 72202

CALIFORNIA
Office of Criminal Justice Planning
7171 Bowling Drive, Suite 210
Sacramento, California 95823

COLORADO
Division of Criminal Justice
Juvenile Justice Specialist
1313 Sherman Street, Room 419
Denver, Colorado 80203

CONNECTICUT
Connecticut Justice Commission
75 Elm Street
Hartford, Connecticut 06115

DELAWARE
Delaware Agency to Reduce Crime
State Office Building
820 North French Street
Wilmington, Delaware 19801

DISTRICT OF COLUMBIA
Office of Criminal Justice Plans and Analysis
Munsey Building, Room 200
1329 E. Street N.W.
Washington, D.C. 20004

FLORIDA
Bureau of Criminal Justice Planning and Assistance
530 Carlton Building Room 215
Tallahassee, Florida 32304

GEORGIA
State Crime Commission
3400 West Peachtree Street N.E.
Atlanta, Georgia 30326

HAWAII
State Law Enforcement and Juvenile Delinquency
Planning Agency
Kamamalu Building, Room 412
1010 Richards Street
Honolulu, Hawaii 96813

IDAHO
Law Enforcement Planning Commission
State Office Building
700 West State Street
Boise, Idaho 83706

ILLINOIS
Illinois Law Enforcement Commission
120 South Riverside Plaza, 10th Floor
Chicago, Illinois 60606

INDIANA
Indiana Criminal Justice Planning Agency
215-17 North Senate Avenue
Indianapolis, Indiana 46202

IOWA
Iowa Crime Commission
Lucas State Office Building
Des Moines, Iowa 50319

KANSAS
Governor's Committee on Criminal Administration
503 Kansas Avenue
Topeka, Kansas 66603

KENTUCKY
Executive Office of Staff Services
Kentucky Department of Justice
State Office Building Annex
Frankfort, Kentucky 40601

LOUISIANA
Louisiana Commission on Law Enforcement
and Administration of Criminal Justice
1885 Wooddale Boulevard, Room 615
Baton Rouge, Louisiana 70806

MAINE
Maine Criminal Justice Planning and Assistance Agency
11 Parkwood Drive
Augusta, Maine 04330

MARYLAND
Governor's Commission on Law Enforcement
and Administration of Justice
One Investment Plaza
Towsen, Maryland 21204

MASSACHUSETTS
Committee on Criminal Justice
110 Tremont Street, 4th Floor
Boston, Massachusetts 02108

MICHIGAN
Office of Criminal Justice Programs
P.O. Box 30026
Lewis Cass Building, Second Floor
Lansing, Michigan 48909

MINNESOTA
Governor's Commission on Crime Prevention
and Control
444 Lafayette Road
St. Paul, Minnesota 55101

MISSISSIPPI
Mississippi Criminal Justice Planning Division
723 North President Street, Suite 400
Jackson, Mississippi 39202

MISSOURI
Missouri Council on Criminal Justice
P.O. Box 1041
Jefferson City, Missouri 65101

MONTANA
Board of Crime Control
1336 Helena Avenue
Helena, Montana 59601

NEBRASKA
Nebraska Commission on Law Enforcement
and Criminal Justice
State Capitol Building
Lincoln, Nebraska 68509

NEVADA
Nevada Commission on Crime
Delinquency and Corrections
State Capitol Building
Carson City, Nevada 89710

NEW HAMPSHIRE
Governor's Commission on Crime and Delinquency
G.A.A. Plaza, Building 3
169 Manchester Street
Concord, New Hampshire 03301

NEW JERSEY
State Law Enforcement Planning Agency
3535 Quaker Bridge Road
Trenton, New Jersey 08625

NEW MEXICO
Department of Criminal Justice
113 Washington Avenue N.W.
Sante Fe, New Mexico 87501

NEW YORK
State of New York, Division of Criminal Justice Services
Office of Planning and Program Assistance
80 Centre Street, Fourth Floor
New York, New York 10013

NORTH CAROLINA
Division of Law and Order
North Carolina Department of Natural and Economic Resources
P.O. Box 27687
Raleigh, North Carolina 27611

NORTH DAKOTA
North Dakota Combined Law Enforcement Council
Box B
Bismark, North Dakota 58505

OHIO
Ohio Department of Economic & Community Development
Administration of Justice Division-JJ Staff, 26th Floor
30 East Broad Street
Columbus, Ohio 43215

OKLAHOMA
Oklahoma Crime Commission
3033 North Walnut
Oklahoma City, Oklahoma 73105

OREGON
Law Enforcement Council
2001 Front Street N.E.
Salem, Oregon 97310

PENNSYLVANIA
Pennsylvania Commission on Crime and Delinquency
Bureau of Planning

P.O. Box 1167
Federal Square Station
Harrisburg, Pennsylvania 17120

PUERTO RICO
Puerto Rico Crime Commission
GPO Box 1256
San Juan, Puerto Rico 00936

RHODE ISLAND
Governor's Justice Commission
110 Eddy Street
East Providence, Rhode Island 02903

SOUTH CAROLINA
Office of Criminal Justice Programs
Edgar A. Brown State Office Building
1205 Pendleton Street
Columbia, South Carolina 29201

SOUTH DAKOTA
Division of Law Enforcement Assistance
200 West Pleasant Drive
Pierre, South Dakota 57501

TENNESSEE
Tennessee Law Enforcement Planning Agency
Browning-Scott Building
4950 Linbar Drive
Nashville, Tennessee 37211

TEXAS
Criminal Justice Division,
Office of the Governor
411 West Thirteenth Street
Austin, Texas 78701

UTAH
Utah Council on Criminal Justice Administration
255 South Third Street, East
Salt Lake City, Utah 84111

VERMONT
Vermont Commission on the Administration of Justice
149 State Street
Montpelier, Vermont 05602

VIRGINIA
Division of Justice and Crime Prevention
8501 Maryland Drive
Richmond, Virginia 23229

WASHINGTON
Division of Criminal Justice
Office of Financial Management
102 North Quince
Olympia, Washington 98504

WEST VIRGINIA
Governor's Committee on Crime, Delinquency & Correction
Morris Square, Suite 321
1212 Lewis Street
Charleston, West Virginia 25301

WISCONSIN
Wisconsin Council on Criminal Justice
122 West Washington
Madison, Wisconsin 53703

WYOMING
Governor's Planning Committee on Criminal Administration
State Office Building, East
Cheyenne, Wyoming 82002

SUGGESTIONS FOR FURTHER READING

Bartollas, C., and Miller, S. J. *The Juvenile Offender.* Rockleigh, N.J.: Allyn and Bacon, 1978.

Carter, Robert M., and Klein, Malcolm W. *Back on the Street: The Diversion of Juvenile Offenders.* Englewood Cliffs, N.J.: Prentice-Hall, 1976.

Ferdinand, Theodore N., editor, *Juvenile Delinquency: Little Brother Grows Up.* Beverly Hills, Cal.: Sage Publications, 1977.

Goldstein, Joseph; Freud, Anna; and Solnit, Albert J. *Before the Best Interests of the Child.* New York: Free Press, 1980.
——————. *Beyond the Best Interests of the Child.* New York: Free Press, 1980.

Haskins, James. *Street Gangs: Yesterday and Today.* New York: Hastings House, 1974.

Hyde, Margaret O. *Foster Care and Adoption*. New York: Franklin Watts, 1982.

_____. *Crime Victims*. New York: Franklin Watts, 1982.

_____. *Crime and Justice in Our Time*. New York: Franklin Watts, 1980.

_____. *Cry Softly: The Story of Child Abuse*. Philadelphia, PA: Westminster Press, 1980.

_____. *My Friend Wants to Run Away*. New York: McGraw-Hill, 1979.

James, Howard. *The Little Victims: How America Treats Its Children*. New York: David McKay, 1975.

Prescott, Peter. *The Child Savers: Juvenile Justice Observed*. New York: Alfred Knopf, 1981.

Sandhu, Harjit S., and Heasley, C. Wayne. *Improving Juvenile Justice*. New York: Human Sciences Press, 1981.

Sarri, Rosemary, and Hasenfeld, Yeheskel. *Brought to Justice? Juveniles, the Courts and the Law*. Ann Arbor, Mich.: The University of Michigan, National Assessment of Juvenile Corrections, 1974.

Sorrentino, Joseph N. *The Concrete Cradle: An Exploration of Juvenile Crime: Its Causes and Cures*. Los Angeles, Cal.: Wollstonecraft, 1975.

_____. *How to Organize the Neighborhood for Delinquency Prevention*. New York: Human Sciences Press, 1979.

Vachss, Andrew H., and Bakal, Yitzhak. *The Life-style Violent Juvenile*. Lexington, Mass.: D. C. Health, 1981.

Vedder, Clyde B. *Juvenile Offenders.* Springfield, Ill.: Charles C. Thomas, 1979.

Wooden, Kenneth. *Weeping in the Playtime of Others: The Plight of Incarcerated Children.* New York: McGraw-Hill, 1976.

INDEX

ABOUT THE AUTHOR

Margaret O. Hyde was born in Philadelphia, Pennsylvania. After graduating from Beaver College, she earned her M.A. degree at Columbia University and was later awarded an honorary Doctor of Letters by Beaver College. She was head of the Science Department at the Shipley School in Bryn Mawr, Pennsylvania.

She has published over thirty-five books, including *Crime and Justice in Our Time* and *Foster Care and Adoption* for young readers. She has also written several documentaries for national television.

Margaret O. Hyde and her husband live in Vermont, where she enjoys skiing and sailing.